Introduction
to Modern Food
and
Beverage Service

INTRODUCTION
TO MODERN FOOD
AND
BEVERAGE SERVICE

WILLIAM L. KAHRL
Food Industry Planning

Prentice-Hall, Inc., Englewood Cliffs, New Jersey

Library of Congress Cataloging in Publication Data

Kahrl, William L
    Introduction to modern food and beverage service.
    (Prentice-Hall series in foodservice management)
    Includes index.
    1. Food service. I. Title.
TX911.K23   642'.5   75-29259
ISBN 0-13-488270-9

Printed in the United States of America

10 9 8 7 6 5 4 3 2 1

Prentice-Hall International, Inc., London
Prentice-Hall of Australia, Pty. Limited, Sydney
Prentice-Hall of Canada, Ltd., Toronto
Prentice-Hall of India Private Limited, New Delhi
Prentice-Hall of Japan, Inc., Tokyo
Prentice-Hall of South-East Asia Private Limited, Singapore

Contents

2

Similarity in All Segments   21

3

Career and Experience   37

4

Control   51

5

Merchandising   73

6

Buying, Storing, and Handling   *91*

7

Food Preparation   *107*

8

Food and Beverage Service   *127*

14

Outside Assistance

15

Planning and Equipment

Appendix   *273*

Index   *295*

Foreword

This is the first of two textbooks designed solely for the food and beverage industry. The second will be *Advanced Modern Food and Beverage Service* and will be for those who have completed the introductory course or for people with some actual experience who wish to further their careers.

In the past, most texts and courses have combined food and beverage service with another activity, like hotels, or limited the coverage to restaurants only. These books will confine themselves to the food service industry only, but will cover all the many segments of the industry.

Unlike the contents of most existing texts, which describe this industry as a very complex field, the information presented here will be more in tune with modern methods and systems—practical, based on many years of operating and planning, and aimed at simplification and a better understanding of the industry. The positive approach will be used throughout both books: Definite suggestions and recommendations will be given in all phases, and the "what not to do"

will be eliminated. Sound, easy-to-understand operating procedures will be stressed; it is essential to learn what to do now
and in the future, rather than to learn the negative aspects.
The main purpose of the text will be to lessen the confusion
that exists in the minds of many and to encourage as many as
possible to choose an excellent career in the food service
industry.

Many of the ideas and methods proposed have not yet
been accepted or put into effect throughout most of the industry, but it is important that we set them forth for the
future. It is difficult to make giant strides in an industry as
large and varied as that of food service, but we must begin to
take steps forward now if we are to correct the many deficiencies that exist. That the ideas to be put forth are sound can be
shown by the many successful operations that have already
started to make changes in their procedures and methods. The
great number of failures, and the wide spread in selling prices,
profits, and losses within the industry; are evidence that
changes are needed. The fact is, we should have started
sooner on new programs. We have all the tools needed to do a
much better job; it is just a matter of getting people to accept
and use them.

Material presented in both these books will apply to
all the various branches of the industry, even including the
smaller facilities. It is important to realize that although this is
a very large industry in total, it is made up of hundreds of
thousands of small places. Many of these do not have the
means to make large improvements, but all can start on a
program of some sort to improve their position in the future.
Then, too, trained leadership is needed most by the average
establishment, not the large successful chains, and this will be
the area for most job openings and opportunities in the
future—the main consideration for those who choose a career
in food service.

AIDS FOR INSTRUCTION

As the title indicates, this text has been prepared
specifically for the novice in the food service industry. It has

two aims: The first is to describe the size, importance, and growth potential of the industry, the wide diversification of its branches and subbranches, its great employment potential, both now and in the future, and the opportunities for advancement in the field, especially for trained people.

The second objective is to outline the major features of the business, with emphasis on the retail side. Even in an introductory course, it is possible to cover a good deal of ground here, since modern food and beverage service is relatively uncomplicated, for the abundance of new technical aids and systems has solved many of our problems.

Classroom experience has shown that today's student is interested in food and beverage service of the present and future, rather than the traditional but outdated methods of the past. Therefore, classroom lectures and discussions should revolve around current operations and examples—the booming fast-food facilities, for example, as well as the family restaurants. Students are interested in actual places and names that they can relate to and understand.

The text can be supplemented with current articles and other material from the media, and with field trips to a variety of typical operations to point out features described in the text. And even though the new student may have had little actual experience in the field, he or she is familiar with the food and beverage service industry at least as a customer, so question, answer, and discussion sessions can prove to be very stimulating.

In this text, I have purposely stayed away from the more technical and complicated information, but have aimed instead at teaching the student the basic and simple fundamentals of the business. My own feeling is that if everyone actively engaged in food service knew and practiced these fundamentals, they would have far less trouble. Any student who learns and understands them should be well on the way to a successful career in the food and beverage service industry. The industry certainly needs leaders who clearly understand the business and, above all, have open minds and are willing to observe, analyze, and make changes that are needed.

The text has been arranged to suit every course,

whether it consists of a certain number of sessions or a semester. There are 15 chapters, so that any kind of credit-hour arrangement or calendar can be accommodated.

William L. Kahrl

This text is dedicated to a book. This book was written thousands of years ago. It has been on the best seller list ever since; more books have been written about it than any other book, and it has been translated into more languages than any other book in history. One small quote from this book could solve many employee and customer relations problems; "Do unto others as you would have them do unto you." I would put this book at the very top of reference reading for all. The name of this book? The Bible.

1

Size, Scope, and Opportunity in the Industry

Objectives

This chapter is a generalized view of the food service industry. After reading it carefully, the student should be able to:

1. Comprehend the vast range of activities within the industry.
2. Have some idea of the types of positions available, with a view to setting his or her own goals.

In embarking on any major activity in life, it is always wise to get some idea of what one is getting into. If you were choosing a career in professional sports, the first thing you might do would be to examine the leaders carefully—learn their size, their appeal to the spectators, their possibilities for the future—and the opportunities for you as an individual. Choosing a business career is no different, in that one should know as much as possible about it, including the potential of the particular business and the individual. It is hoped that the information to follow will shed some new light on the food service industry for many who have not looked at the whole picture before.

Most people in the business have been confined to or have worked in only one of the many parts, and have not had the chance to see the entire view—that is, not seeing the forest for the trees. This is truly an industry all in itself that does not need ties to other endeavors in the future.

One of the main problems in the past has been that food service has been considered a minor activity. For years, hotels gave little attention to their food service, assuming that little or no profit could be made in this end, but only in renting the rooms. Food service in hospitals, colleges, schools, industry, and so on, has long been considered a necessary evil, so here, too, it has taken a back seat to the major endeavor. The time has come for us to stand up and say that the food service industry is a profession in itself, and a good one. The people in the past who did take this approach have built fine operations and huge, successful chains, all very profitable and substantial.

SIZE AND SCOPE

Size

Food service is now ranked as the fourth largest industry in the United States, and there are indications that it might deserve even a higher position. In 1972, total volume in eating and drinking places was set at $32.7 billion. Compare this to $23.9 billion for autos, and $19.2 billion for the steel industry. It has been predicted that by the year 1980, the food service industry could reach $65 billion in this country and $200 billion in the world. These figures are averages from many different sources in the industry. Some predict even more growth for eating out in the future, but it is best to present the more reasonable estimates.

In addition to a very substantial growth over the years, it is also interesting to note how the food service industry has fared through depressions and recessions, for in selecting a career it is important to know how your industry will do in difficult times as well as in general prosperity. Even during the very bad Depression of the 1930s, our industry did well as far as sales and employment were concerned. In fact, several of the major chains we know today started during the Depression years and continued to grow through these most difficult times. In the midst of the 1974-5 recession, our industry continued to show gains in sales, and we did not have massive layoffs of employees evidenced in many other industries. Perhaps the emphasis may change during a recession—to lower priced foods and different kinds of service—but the fact that great numbers of people must or prefer to eat out cannot be denied. People can do without a new car or a color television when the going gets rough, but we all must eat, and do it on a regular basis.

The following article headlines and summary of "Eating Out Sales" from *Nation's Restaurant News* (May 26, 1975) show that the food service industry continues to grow and prosper despite a generally gloomy economic picture. In the spring of 1975 the national unemployment figure was estimated by many sources to be in excess of 8,000,000 people—an astounding figure which clearly shows that many other industries are not too "recession proof." In contrast, growth in the food sevice industry in the past ten years alone has been very rapid, and all indications are that this rate will continue in the future, for many sound reasons. This is a most important consideration for anyone choosing a career for the future.

Scope

Another major fact is the wide variety of endeavors within the industry itself. It is not limited to one particular area or single market, thus also giving it great strength and stability. You could be engaged in the manufacture and sale of a very fine single product, but there is always the risk that the demand will drop in the future, or that some new item will replace it. This condition does not exist in the food industry. There may be shifts or changes, but the total potential is there, and will be for a long time to come.

Following is a partial listing of branches of the industry, to point up the great diversity.

Restaurants. Numbering in the hundreds of thousands, restaurants spread throughout the whole country. Although we hear a great deal about the large, successful chains, the majority of these places are still individually owned and operated.

Hotels. One has only to travel to see the huge number of these institutions, and especially the great number of new places built in the past few years. All must provide food and drink for their customers. In fact, many of the newer hotels have several types of food and beverage service, to make sure they satisfy all their guests.

Motels. This idea started many years ago, to meet the needs of the many people traveling by car. The original concept was one of "do-it-yourself"—find your own room, take in the bags, park the car by the front door. But many of the more recently built motels are much like hotels, in that they provide all these services for the guest, and are multistory with elevators. Some of the smaller motels do not offer food and beverage, or do so on only a very limited scale; however, the larger units have found it advantageous to offer good food and beverage service, if only to satisfy the people occupying the rooms.

Resorts. These are often classed with hotels, but there is a difference as far as food service is concerned. Whether it be a ski, sport, or beach resort, food service takes on an even more important function because most guests stay for a longer time than hotel guests do, and being a more or less captive audience, they demand that the food and service be tops.

Clubs. There are many private clubs, and as leisure time increases owing to shorter workweeks and increased interest in activities like golf and tennis, this part of the industry should also flourish. Again, food and beverage service is of major importance to clubs—in fact, many have built up bigger memberships by offering good food.

Schools. Food service here is referred to as the "school lunch program," although it is now being expanded to include breakfast and, in some cases, dinners. Right now, in terms of meals served, this is the largest single branch of the food service industry, even though it is estimated to be providing meals to only about one-third of the students. This part of the industry has only one way to go as far as growth is concerned, and that is *up.*

Colleges. The growth here is not as evident as in other fields, but even if their problems continue in the future, we will always have colleges. Colleges have been among the leaders recently in realizing the importance of good food service for the students. Many have started programs to offer greater variety of more popular foods, redecorate facilities, and do everything else possible to entice students to eat on campus. A remark was made recently that students should look into the food service of various colleges before entering, just as they used to pick a college or university based on the success of its football team.

In-Plant. Sometimes called "industrial feeding," this has been a sizable part of our industry for years and will continue to be so. It can vary from vending machines to elaborate executive dining rooms, complete with bars. Most of these facilities are self-service, and usually at a reduced price to the employees; if there are losses, the parent company subsidizes the food service to make sure it is available. Most consider this a fringe benefit for the plant or company employees and try to do the best job possible. A few companies even offer free meals as an incentive. With many plants and businesses locating away from congested areas in the future, in-plant feeding might also be considered a necessity, since employees will not have the time to drive long distances at lunchtime for their meal.

In-Flite. This is a relative newcomer in our industry, since it is only about 30 years of age. However, this segment has grown by leaps and bounds until it has become a very important part of the whole system. Some airlines have their own feeding installations, while others use contract feeders to supply the meals needed on planes. Many thought that the advent of faster planes would cause a drop in this business, but it has continued to expand, largely because of the public's fast acceptance of this form of travel.

Fast Food. Mostly referred to as the "hamburger business," this is a very large and lucrative part of our industry that has been overlooked by many in the past because they thought it lacked class and distinction. Perhaps this is not elegant dining, but in 1972, the two largest and most profitable companies in the industry were chains of fast-food operations. This segment accounts for most of the franchise activity in the industry. The fact that it can offer food for lower prices, fast service for those in a hurry, the highest dollar income per employee per year, easy job training, excellent controls, and—last but not least—high profit means that it will be with us for a long time to come and continue to be successful. Because most leaders in our industry in the past have overlooked this type of food business, and many have the opinion that it is very simple to operate, not much has appeared in textbooks or in schools about it. However, this text will not only mention this segment, but will treat it with the attention and consideration it deserves.

Armed Services. Up until recently, the feeding of the armed forces was the number one branch of the industry in volume and number of meals served. Even though it has dropped a few notches, it is still a very large part of the industry. In fact, a great deal of research and development is being carried on now by the government to find new methods and ideas to improve the food served. Back a few years, the armed services set up a testing area for food service equipment— checking performances, capacities, and endurance, which had never been done before. Many of the things learned from this research proved to be most helpful to the entire industry. The quality of the food service is recognized as a plus item for better morale of the members, especially in peacetime.

Hospitals. Recent figures put the number of hospitals in excess of 8,000. New units may be built in the future to meet demand, and, of course, many of the existing facilities are being expanded right now to take care of current needs. Each must have food service, not only for the patients but also for the hundreds of employees. One minor point of interest: Several hospitals are experimenting with the service of wine to patients, so some day we may refer to "food and beverage service" in hospitals.

Nursing Homes. This is not a new field, but one that is increasing in size and importance. The shortage of space in hospitals, plus the ever-increasing number of people needing this service, will mean rapid growth in this field.

Feeding the Elderly. Although this has not been a major factor in the past or been given too much consideration, it too could become a sizable task for the industry in the future. The increasing number of senior citizens living on low, fixed incomes is now getting attention from Washington, and new legislation has provided considerable amounts of money to speed this program. There are many problems still to be solved in this area—transportation, where to feed, and so on—but they will be solved, and this will become a large and continuing program for the future.

Correctional Institutions. As of just recently, some in our industry are beginning to notice this segment more closely. There is great need for improvement and help in this direction; several large food service firms are even considering contract service for this feeding, and more attention will be given in the future to the idea of upgrading here. In fact, food training programs in these institutions are being given more serious consideration, both for rehabilitation and to supply much-needed help in our industry in the future.

Food Processing. This is a rapidly expanding part of the whole picture, not only for the retail trade, but for the food service industry as well. The rapid growth in the use of more convenience foods has caused a tremendous increase in the number of food processing plants. This can open up many jobs and opportunities in the future, not only in the manufacturing end but in the sales field. Anyone with good knowledge of the food service industry could certainly fit into this branch.

Commissaries. Many large companies have built and operate their own food processing plants and deliver to all their units on a regular basis. In fact, some have even expanded the market for their products by offering them to other food service facilities in addition to their own places.

Food Suppliers. Naturally, thousands of these—sometimes referred to as purveyors—exist throughout the country. Most deal only with the commercial field, and again, anyone who knows the food service business and its needs could easily fit into this picture in the future.

Equipment Manufacturers. These form a very large and profitable part of the industry, specializing as they do in the manufacture of food service equipment only. One has only to visit any of the large national trade shows each year to get a firsthand look at the potential in this service part of our industry. Most of these companies keep in very close touch with the industry, to keep up to date on what is needed.

Sales Representatives. There are thousands of sales representatives working for the food processing and equipment manufacturers in direct contact with the food service industry. For someone with sales ability and a knowledge of the food service industry, this can be a very fine career.

Designing and Planning. Whether it be the actual drawing of equipment layout plans or making designs for fabricators and manufacturers, there will always be a big demand for people with this ability. As the entire business grows, more planners and designers will be needed to take care of the expansion.

Consulting and Advising. There are many people now in this field who are working solely for the food service industry, and there will be many more in the future as the business and industry grows. This position requires considerable experience and time, but is a very active part of the whole picture. The reason there are so many more consultants in the food service industry than in some of the other major industries, like autos, steel, or oil refining, is that our business, even though large in total, is made up primarily of thousands of smaller facilities. Except for the very large food service chains, these places cannot afford to hire consultants and designers on a full-time basis, so they must use general consultants when the time comes for them to make changes or they need new plans and layouts.

Management Companies. These companies, which offer another area of endeavor, have grown in number, and in size, in recent years in the industry. Most of them do not initiate facilities, but rather are called in to take over the management and running of food service installations. Many college food services are operated by management companies, as are many in-plant cafeterias. However, now these companies are expanding into such areas as school lunches and others, where there is need for some professional management and techniques that cannot be supplied by the facility itself.

We have listed almost two dozen areas within the industry; these are the major parts and will show the great diversification and choice available. Naturally, there is competition among the various branches, just as one restaurant will compete with another. The fast-food place tries to lure the student from the campus or school at lunchtime, and now the schools are fighting back by offering more variety and the kinds of foods students prefer. All this competition is good for us; it is helping the entire industry—the better the food and service, the more people will eat out, which should be the goal in the long run.

Work Choices

In addition to the wide choice of fields listed above, the person with training and skill in the food service industry has some other advantages not to be found in many other large industries. One can select the geographical area desired, even down to specific cities or towns, since food facilities are everywhere. In fact, the choice in this matter is so great that there are those who work in the north in summer and in the south in winter, in order to enjoy good weather all year. In many other industries (an auto plant, steel mill, or appliance manufacturer) you must go to the precise location of the company and its plants; the choice is narrow.

Now there is also a wide choice of hours and days of work. If you are one who would prefer fewer days and shorter hours with more vacation time, you might want to consider the school lunch program, or in-plant feeding, where normally only one meal per day is served five days a week. Or, perhaps you would prefer to work nights and continue your education during the day, or to work part time or only on certain days; such arrangements are easy to find in the food service industry.

It is also an industry where you can select your own work status and better match your desires for the future. Many people want to work for a large company and rise to a high position; others may want to work for a smaller operation and share in the results of their efforts. After a short time of working for someone else, many decide to start their own business, and this is still very possible in the food service industry. If you do not want to go out on a limb by yourself, there is the franchise route, where you are the owner and operator but a larger company provides the plans, systems, national advertising, and other needed help. All these roads are open in this industry and will continue to be in the future. In brief, there are no limits or restrictions other than the ones you place on yourself—you can go just as far and high as you choose in this business.

LEADERSHIP POSITIONS

Most of the course and school titles for our business use the word "management"—Hotel and Motel Management, Food Service Management, and so on. In so doing, they are missing the point that there are many fine positions of leadership in the industry other than manager. Of course, all of us have a desire to be the top administrator or manager some day, but we should not overlook the other good jobs available. The same mistake is made by many, both in our business and out, who think the manager and owner of the elegant gourmet dining establishment must make the most money. Although there are some that have, there has been a lot more money made in the so-called hamburger business over the years.

Other than manager, there are many challenging and well-paid jobs in the food service industry.

Assistant Manager

Depending on the size of the operation, it is possible that this category will present great opportunities for many in our business. Not only does this position offer an excellent chance to learn, but it is the stepping-stone to the eventual goal of management.

Eating-out sales increase over '74

WASHINGTON—Total eating and drinking place sales continued well ahead of early 1974's pace the first three months of this year, the U.S. Dept. of Commerce reported.

The totals for January, February and March respectively were $3.43 million, $3.28 million and $3.75 million, compared with $3.0 million, $2.87 million and $3.23 million for the same months last year. (Food service sales traditionally drop off in February and then rise sharply.)

Virtually all the increases can be attributed to inflationary menu price hikes and new units rather than any rise in real sales.

Meanwhile, a just-released Bureau of Labor Statistics survey based on 1972-73 figures indicates that families were spending an average of $8.15, or 27% of a total weekly $30.32 average food expenditures on food away from home. Presumably the other 73% was going for supermarket and grocery store expenditures. The eating out proportion rose steadily through the 1960s and early 1970s as more food service units opened.

The survey also showed that families in the lower income groups spent about 6% of their total incomes on food away from home and in the highest income groups, a 3.4% average.

No figures are available since mid-1973, although industry officials believe that as much as one-third of all food

Higher traffic, sales
Industry leaders see upward trend

IFMA: Industry holds own in rough economic climate

Food Service Manager

In the future, we will still have the chefs and people in charge of food preparation, but more and more facilities in the business are now seeking competent people who can supervise what we will call food service. We all know that correct preparation of a food item is important, but even more important is how and when it reaches the customer, and that is the job of the food service manager. This person has great influence on the amount of business done. If he or she is competent, service will be faster, the paying guest will be more satisfied, and, in general, the operation will do better.

Purchasing

This has always been a very important function and will continue to be so in the future. In view of the total amount of sales in the industry and the amount of food and other materials that must be bought to transact that business, there can be little doubt that this function will remain vital and will afford some good positions.

Accounting and Control

This position is becoming a more important aspect of our industry each day, because no one will be successful in the future without control. This function will go beyond accounting as we knew it in the past; we must know not only what *has happened*, but what *is happening* and *will happen* in the future. It can be compared to the early days of aviation, when most flew "by the seat of their pants," hoping that they would get where they were headed, or even that they would be able to reach the ground safely. Now, most of the guesswork has been removed from flying, and we in the food service industry are accomplishing the same goal—we can tell where we are now and where we are headed.

Supervision and Training

As food service companies become larger, there is more and more need for competent supervision. This position has also changed, from the older version—someone who rode around to see if the floors and rest rooms were clean—to highly trained people who can detect problems and solve them on the spot.

Food Serving Manager

Throughout this text, we will divide the industry into three segments: food preparation, food service—the process of getting the food to the people who serve it—and food serving. We need this breakdown because there is more to the business than just cooking a pot of stew. In fact, we have learned that there is a great deal more to success in our business than the cooking, and this is why food serving has assumed a more important role; unless we can get the product to the paying consumer right and make him happy, all the cooking skill in the world will be of little value. For those with years of experience in the business, this area is comparable to the "hostess," or "maitre d'," but the new concept goes far beyond these two older descriptions.

Associated Industries

Above and beyond the food service industry, which is already a giant and growing daily, there will be many more careers and jobs open in the associated industries, or support fields, as many call them. These include such industries as equipment manufacturers, food processors, food brokers, supply companies, design and layout companies, repair and maintenance, management companies, and many more fields of endeavor needed to support our industry. Anyone who has had training in and understands the food service industry will be qualified for many fine positions in these allied fields as well. Years ago, anyone could sell equipment in our industry, but now, with the advanced technology in equipment, the good salesman must know something about the business itself. In many cases, he or she must be able even to demonstrate the piece of equipment and prove that it is a good investment. In short, in all these allied fields, it has now become necessary to know what our industry needs or will need; to fulfill this requirement takes some knowledge of the industry itself.

In other words, there will be many fine, well-paid positions open in the future for anyone with training and skill. We can't all become the boss, but it is reassuring to know that there are many more jobs available with challenge and good pay. On behalf of Women's Liberation, it must be noted that very few industries have as many women in top positions as has food service; in certain branches, women managers far outnumber men, and rightly so, because they are doing a good job. As you can see, there is opportunity for all.

PROJECTION OF INDUSTRY GROWTH

Not only are you entering a very diversified industry, with a choice of location, hours of work, and many kinds of endeavor, but you have the opportunity of being associated with one of the fastest-growing industries in the country. Some parts of the industry may not grow as fast as others, but the total increase in the number of people eating away from home will certainly rise. It has been estimated that we now eat one out of four meals away from home, and this will increase in the future. Our society is *on the move*, whether it be for business or pleasure, which means that people are away from home more at mealtimes and thus forced to eat out more often. There have been many predictions as to the total increase in the away-from-home feeding market for the coming years. Total-dollar yearly figures estimated run from approximately $40 billion in 1974 to perhaps $80 billion a year in the early 1980s.

That the industry will expand is certain; the forms that the expansion will take may, however, surprise us. For example, there are indications that, in the future, more varieties of food service will be established. Catering, for instance, could be expanded soon; if it becomes more difficult for the customers to come to us, perhaps further ways and means will be found to take the prepared foods to people.

In addition, there will undoubtedly be shifts in size and emphasis among the various segments of the industry. There may well be fewer to feed in the armed forces, but this could be offset by the need to feed many more of the elderly, or schoolchildren. Because of the energy crisis, highway locations might suffer a loss of sales, but this could mean an increase in business for downtown locations and local facilities. College feeding might decrease, but in-plant could become much larger in an effort to save on fuel. After all,

Wow! 250,000 jobs

In spite of high national unemployment figures, there are 250,000 job openings each year in the foodservice industry, including 25,000 for managers and supervisors, reports a midwestern management newsletter.

An industry spokesman is quoted as predicting that the industry plans to spend $1.3 million for enlisting and training people for these jobs. Another industry executive estimates that the foodservice industry will expand within 10 years to $100 billion a year and employ four million employees.

According to the newsletter, industry executives are helping design educational training programs at colleges and high schools for future employees.

Keep it clean

Learning how to keep a kitchen clean is just as important as serving good food. Now everyone can learn about sanitation—at home, through industry associations and companies, and at colleges and universities.

National Institute for the Foodservice Industry (NIFI) has released the first of 16 foodservice management courses called "Applied Foodservice Sanitation." Course includes a hard cover textbook in addition to a course book for home study and a student and instructor's manual for industry group training and classroom study.

Course has been reviewed by the Food Service Branch of the Food and Drug Administration in Washington, D.C., the National Environmental Health Association, and the National Restaurant Association.

Source: *Food Management*, April 1974.

people in the future may not buy as many large cars, but this will mean only that the major auto companies will change to smaller, more economical models.

In brief, the total market for feeding will be here in the future in one form or another. This is why it is important for textbooks and all formal types of training or teaching to cover all segments of our industry, instead of just a few, as has been done in the past. Electrical engineers once found plenty of jobs in the space program and defense plants, but that changed, and most new graduates were forced to seek other work; many were hired by the utility companies, which have had a terrific growth. In the same way, graduates of any food service program should have knowledge of all parts so that they too can change with the conditions. Anyone trained only in what was known as "car service" would have trouble finding a job now, because this type of food service has become almost extinct.

Another feature to consider is that food is one commodity that everyone must have—we can do without many of the products now being sold, but we all must eat to live. Although many are predicting the economic future for our country and the rest of the world, no one actually knows what will happen in the future, as we can see from many of the forecasts made in the past. The food service industry now is in a good position to weather almost any kind of business climate in the future. If we could open and operate restaurants in the depths of the Depression of the 1930s without knowing what we were doing, it should be possible to do much better in the future.

In contrast to many years ago, we now have all the know-how—systems, methods, support, and tools—to do a good job in the future. All that is needed now is a change from "can't be done" to "will do," and many of our problems will be much smaller.

SUMMARY

1. *Size of the Industry.* The food service industry is the fourth largest in the United States and a major business worldwide as well. In addition to the importance of size, the fact that it is so widespread geographically adds many advantages that many other industries do not have.

2. *Diversification.*   Twenty-three branches or segments of the industry were listed in this chapter. This great diversification is not only a stabilizing feature for the entire industry, but gives the people working in the industry a great choice for their future careers.

3. *Future Growth.* Despite any general business predictions, it is evident from all sources that the industry will

continue to grow and expand at a high rate. There may be shifts within the framework, as there might be in all businesses, but the overall picture is very bright.

4. *Need for Greater Efficiency.* There is a dire need right now, and certainly will be in the future, for improvements in all areas of the entire food service industry. We must become more efficient, increase productivity in all branches, get ready to meet higher costs for all materials and wages, and think more about ways to hold our prices in line instead of continuing to pass off our inefficiency in the form of ever-increasing prices to the customers.

5. *Need for Skilled Leadership.* To handle this future growth and make all the changes that will be needed, there can be little doubt that the industry will need and be looking for new and better trained workers in the future. We will need trained men and women who know efficiency and productivity, are willing to try new systems and methods, and have the imagination and creativity to put an end to our biggest problem—"This is the way we have always done it!"

QUESTIONS FOR REVIEW

1. List five of the branches of the food service industry, with at least one important fact about each.

2. Which segment of the industry, from the brief descriptions given in this chapter, seems to appeal to you most right now? Why?

3. What is the importance of the function of accounting and control to the food service industry?

4. In what directions is the industry expected to advance in the future?

2

Similarity in All Segments

Objectives

In this chapter, we shall look at the factors that are common to all branches of the food service industry. When the student completes the chapter, he should understand:

1. The interrelationship of the many branches of the food service industry.
2. The basic principles common to all segments.
3. The advantages of the similarities between segments.

In visiting and studying all the various areas and kinds of operations that make up the total food service industry, one gets a first impression that they are vastly different. In fact, the owners and managers in different segments are apt to insist that the type of food service they offer is very different from all the others, is more difficult, has many more problems. But after years of experience in dealing with all these variations, the realization finally comes that there is a common thread woven into all, and that they are not so different after all. Suddenly, one sees that they all have the same basic functions and problems, and all are in the same business—serving food and beverages to people.

It is unfortunate that this feeling of difference has existed to such a degree for so long, because otherwise, much more progress could have been made throughout the entire industry. A good salesman with ability and know-how can sell any product; this is proved every day as the top salespeople move from company to company and product to product and still are successful. The same condition exists in our business: A capable leader who produces good results in one branch of food service won't take long to achieve the same fine performance in another branch; food-preparation productivity studies can help produce a better cook in any type of facility.

Many in our business, however, continue within the narrow confines of their particular type of service without even taking a look at any other segment. Even the trade magazines in the past were mostly aimed at only one type of service—fast food, hospitals, schools, cafeterias, restaurants,

23

or hotels (which would not even include motels)—without trying to reach more of the industry, but now they are beginning to broaden their markets.

Having worked in all fields and spent years with large chains that were engaged in varied interests in food service, I can testify that they are all very much alike. In reading a large number of trade magazines regularly, even though they concentrate on certain areas, one can see clearly that the ideas and suggestions that are good for one branch can often be applied successfully to another. This chapter will be devoted to showing just how much alike they are, and to furthering the idea that our training and education should be aimed at equipping people to go into any segment they choose.

TRANSITIONS WITHIN THE INDUSTRY

Every successful manager applies the same basic principles of management to his operation. This is what we in the food service industry must do in the future—establish good, standard, basic principles of operation, apply them, and follow through, no matter what we call the service. This particularly pertains to the interesting transitions that have been and still are occurring in our industry, as noted below.

Automat to Vending

The basic principles and idea for much of our modern vending machines for food and beverages came from the "automat" operations started many years ago.

French Service to Display Cooking

Even though the practice of cooking and serving at the table has become difficult for many to continue, this showmanship has been retained to a degree by the use of what are called display kitchens, visible to the patrons who can sit at their tables and watch the steaks being broiled.

Greater Productivity from Fast Food

Since it was learned that some of the fast-food operations were producing more dollar sales per employee than were many of the higher-priced food service operations, quite a few of the efficient procedures used by the fast-food operations have been brought over to table service.

Control System from Car Service

The first pre-ring registers were originally developed for car service, because of the need to speed service and assist the large number of young, untrained servers. A preprinted check was inserted into a register that rang the sales, totaled them, and recorded the sales of each server, who could then pay later. Now we have a more sophisticated, computer-type system that can do the same thing for table-service operations, plus record and total the sales of individual items automatically.

Equipment Testing by the Armed Services

Years ago, the armed services set up a test center for the various kinds of equipment used in food service. The results of this research greatly improved many pieces of equipment now being used by all the branches of the industry.

Better Sanitation from Hospitals

The hospitals were the early leaders in better methods of cleaning, sterilization, and guarding against contamination, and now we find these same practices adopted in all segments of food service.

Portion Control from Moderate-Priced Restaurants

Although most people now know about the value of accurate portion control, many years ago this was not widely used. With the advent of more moderate-priced restaurants serving large numbers of people, it became necessary to put in a rigid portion-control system to maintain the profit level.

Elaborate Buffets from Cafeterias

Many of the finer food service operations are now featuring attractive buffet service, or combining it with their regular table service, to increase volume and sales. This, of course, is an adaptation of the early cafeteria-type self-service.

Prepared Food from Large Chains

When the time came for many of the smaller chains to expand and open more units, it was realized that there would be a problem in obtaining hundreds of capable chefs and cooks to maintain a uniform quality level of food, and this fact prompted the establishment of commissaries where the food was prepared and sent out to facilities for serving. As the distribution points became more widespread, the need for freezing arose, and thus the many large processors specializing in this service came into being.

Recipes from Large Chains

Early commercial cookery was a more or less hit-and-miss process controlled by one man who had the secret recipe and list of ingredients. Then it was realized that a complete set of controlled-quality recipes were needed to insure uniformity. These recipes, developed and tested in the kitchens of the large chains, soon became available to all in the industry.

Food Service in Motels from Hotels

The early motels had little or no food service of their own. Guests would be referred to a "good eating place down the road." But in a short while, the motel managements saw that they needed to install their own food service, just as the hotels did many years before.

Tight Controls from Low-Cost Operations

Many of the ideas relating to close control and careful budgeting, now widespread through all parts of the industry, came first from those who were forced to provide food on a limited amount of money per meal or day.

Commissary to Wholesale to Retail

Some of the large chains with commissaries soon learned that they had additional potential markets in supplying food to other operations and selling their most popular products to the retail market.

Limited Menu from Fast Food

The early menus used were very elaborate and carried a long list of entrees at each meal. The feeling was that there should be something on the menu to please each and every taste. It was the fast-food element that first realized this not only was costly but resulted in slow service, and they immediately reduced the number of items being offered at any one time. The idea was successful, and now most menus are more limited.

Seating and Decor in Self-Service Fast Food

The original fast-food self-service facilities had a window where the food was handed out to the customers standing in line. The customer had a choice of sitting at a table outside, eating in his car, or taking the food home. This system has also been modified; many of these places now offer attractive air-conditioned dining areas where the customer can eat in comfort after getting the food. This is an instance in which fast food took an idea from the finer eating establishments.

In-Flite Feeding to Hospitals

Some of the methods and ideas used in feeding passengers on airplanes are now being adapted to the feeding of patients in hospitals.

These are but a few examples of how all the segments of the industry are interrelated. They point up the fact that each can learn much from the other and adapt good features that will be beneficial. The interesting thing to note is that the ideas can go in either direction. For instance, one large chain of moderate-priced, fast-service restaurants hired a very famous chef. Soon he had introduced many of his famous dishes in hundreds of locations throughout the nation. The important thing in the future is that we look at all types of food service; by adopting the best ideas from each, every branch of the industry will benefit.

FUNDAMENTAL PRINCIPLES FOR ALL SEGMENTS

As further proof of the similarity among all types of food service, one has only to look at some of the very large and successful food chains today. Some are in all types of service— fast food, gourmet, in-plant, hospital, commissary, retail and wholesale sales, designing and planning, hotels, motels, bars, lounges, colleges, cafeterias, and so on. There must be a common denominator to success in our industry, or these companies could not operate such a wide range of activities and be successful. If you consider the variety of services that a large hotel must offer its guests now—bars, lounges, coffee shop, gourmet dining, employees' cafeteria, room service, banquets, parties, buffets—it is easy to see that there is a common thread running through all these seemingly diversified activities.

The lesson to learn here is that there are fundamental operational principles that apply to all and must be practiced no matter what the service or type of facility. Once one has learned and practiced these basics, he may enter any part of the industry and be successful. Following is a list of these basics that are needed. They will all be explained in more detail later in the text, but for now it is important to identify them.

Good Planning

All facilities today must be carefully planned for efficient and productive food service. Product, work, and people flow are now set up to ensure the minimum waste of effort, motion, and steps. We do not and will not in the future have an abundance of low-priced labor to offset poor planning and layout.

Menus and Merchandising

A good menu, whether it be printed or on a board, must be made first, because this is what determines or sets the pattern for so many of the other factors important to the operation. The menu must fit the market, the facility, and the ability of the employees if the operation is to succeed. Even poor quality food and bad service can be directly traced to the menu itself in many instances. The wrong menu can be compared to a factory set up to produce transistor radios and then switched to the manufacture of riding mowers.

Purchasing

Not only must all food, beverages, and supplies be bought to careful specifications in order to ensure quality, but careful thought must be given to how the products will be used, prepared, and served. Will the facility prepare all foods from scratch, or buy certain prepared foods? Will all butchering be done on the premises, or will fabricated cuts be bought ready for use? Will there be extensive baking, or will some of the new frozen, ready-to-bake products be utilized? These decisions must be made, because of their profound effect on all parts of the operation.

Receiving

In view of the huge amount of money spent for food, beverages, and other supplies, the best possible facilities and systems should be provided for careful receiving of this merchandise. It has been estimated that less than 40 percent of the food service facilities in the industry have adequate receiving facilities and systems.

Storage

Many neglect this very important function; this can be seen by personal observation of existing facilities. Not only do most fail to have the proper storage—cool for dry stores, ample refrigerated space for perishables, enough capacity for frozen—but they do not even have proper shelving. The result is either an excessive number of deliveries, which can be costly as to price and all the additional work at the location, or much waste and loss because of the difficulty in handling and counting.

Issuing

Even without a full-time issue clerk, it is possible to install some sort of system in issuing food and supplies to the various departments. Anything would be better than having many people making hundreds of trips each day in and out of bulk-storage areas that should be secured most of the time. In addition to the possible material loss, think of all of the wasted steps and motion involved in such a system.

When considering the daily supplies of food to all departments we must think in terms of two types of storage: *bulk* and *point of use*. Bulk storage is confined to the major areas such as storerooms, walk-in refrigerators, and freezers. Normally these are located at the rear near the receiving areas. In these places you store foods and materials in cases and boxes. Point of use storage consists of reach-in refrigerators, freezers, mobile racks, and shelving located throughout the operation. The proper procedure is to issue daily from bulk to point of use stations. This stops all of those needless trips to bulk storage areas during operating periods. In fact, if the point of use storage is adequate, the bulk storage areas can be locked for most of the time to help in the matter of security.

Security

Some recent estimates have placed the industry's loss due to pilferage as high as 7.5 percent of gross business. Again, all segments of the industry have this problem and must do everything possible to reduce this loss.

Food Preparation

All segments must prepare the food for service, and the procedures are the same. This job is no easier or more difficult for one branch of the industry than for another.

Food Service

Once the food is prepared, the same general principles must be followed to see that it is served properly. Whether the entree goes on a cafeteria line or is served at a table, the same rules of proper handling must be observed.

Beverage Service

There are standard methods for proper beverage service, and these also must be observed to the letter.

Proper Equipment

This is a very important consideration to all now, because the equipment used by the industry must replace a lot of the skilled help no longer available in so many operations. It is true that we operated for years with very poor and inefficient equipment, but we did have one other thing going for us that has disappeared—a lot of inexpensive skilled help who could handle this type of equipment.

Control

Most commonly called accounting, control now goes a great deal further in modern food service. Without having the best system possible to know what one is doing and what is happening at all times, it will be difficult to operate successfully.

Warehandling

This is the largest single function, taking the most effort, in food service. Included in warehandling are the washing of pots, pans, utensils, china, trays, flatware, glasses, and so on. The washing might seem like a big job, but the proper handling, which includes getting the ware to the washer and back to points of use, is by far the most difficult part of the job.

Labor Utilization

A most severe problem for all today in food service is labor utilization. Not only is there a shortage of skilled employees, but it is difficult to hire even the unskilled. Everyone has the problem of hiring, training, excessive labor turnover, and low employee productivity. No matter what type of operation one visits, the first difficulty mentioned by management is the shortage of help.

Reducing Costs

Cost reduction relates also to increasing profits or reducing losses, but no matter how it is described, everyone is faced with this problem constantly.

Sanitation

The problem of sanitation is of particular importance to our industry because we are selling a product that is consumed by the public, and, of course, there can be serious problems from lack of cleanliness. This too has become more difficult because of the shortage of help.

Safety

The large number of accidents in the food service industry indicates that we have some dangerous working conditions still existing that will need correction.

Maintenance

Maintenance of both plant and equipment continues to be a big problem as well as a costly one. Because we are using more sophisticated equipment, preventive maintenance has become even more difficult.

Decor and Atmosphere

Pleasant surroundings for the consumer have become a very essential feature in all parts of the industry. Facilities in schools, colleges, plants, and even correctional institutions are now paying more attention to the appearance of the dining areas than they did in the past.

Laws, Codes, and Ordinances

Not only are all segments of the industry subject to many laws already on the books, but many new ones are being made each day that will affect everyone.

Energy Conservation

We are a very large industry and use a huge amount of energy, so there can be little doubt that much must be done to reduce the amount used in the future. At the present time, we do waste a lot of energy; efforts to end this waste will help to reduce operating costs, as well as conserve the energy itself.

Customer Satisfaction

Whether one is feeding a school lunch to an eighth grader or a gourmet dinner to a business tycoon, pleasing the public is the same. All customers are looking for good food, prompt and efficient service, reasonable prices, and a pleasant atmosphere for dining.

Convenience Foods

Slowly but surely, we are all beginning to see the advantages of using as much preprepared and ready foods as possible, although this idea was limited to only a very few parts of the business years ago. The large packers and processors are beginning to realize that this is a total market; they are performing such services as preparing special diet foods for hospitals along with the regular items they offer.

Despite the many seemingly different types of feeding within the entire food service industry, we are finally beginning to realize that there is a great deal of similarity. The objectives are the same, and certainly the difficulties and problems are very much alike. The more all realize this fact, the better it will be for the entire industry because we can then start to work together, pooling and combining knowledge and skills to improve the total effort. It is most important that the newcomer to the industry understand this similarity, because it opens up a much broader field of opportunity for him than existed in the past. Instead of his being committed to one limited field, which he may find not to his liking after a while, he can know that there are many other opportunities available to someone with his training.

A very capable manager in the restaurant field who tires of that work could transfer to school feeding, and become very content in the new position. A person managing some very fine feeding operations for a chain of department stores could change to the fast-food field of endeavor to make more money.

The more the various segments do interchange management and talent in the future, the better it will be for the industry, because very often good ideas from one segment will be carried to another, benefitting it and the individual.

SUMMARY

1. *Same Business.* The common thread linking all branches of the food service industry is that all are in the busi-

ness of providing food and beverages to people. As a result, their basic functions and problems are the same.

2. *Advantages of Similarity.* Because of the basic similarity of all segments, workers in each are capable of transferring to any other without difficulty. In addition, ideas for improvement can flow between segments, to the benefit of all. Many such ideas have made their way from one segment to others, and are now common practice throughout the industry.

3. *Training of Managers.* Students of the industry should be well trained in its fundamentals, rather than confining their education to one field, so that they can take advantage of the opportunities offered by any or all branches, both when they enter the industry and later, if they feel the need for change.

4. *Basic Principles.* Some of these fundamentals that must be learned by the student are in the areas of planning, merchandising, purchasing, receiving and issuing, preparation and service, labor utilization, and control.

QUESTIONS FOR REVIEW

1. Name some of the practices used in food service today that originated in segments other than the ones now using them most.

2. What kind of decisions must be made regarding the function of purchasing?

3. Why is sanitation a problem of great importance to the food service industry?

4. How do modern control systems in restaurants benefit from a practice started in a now-obsolete branch of the industry?

3

Career and Experience

Objectives

This chapter explains the current and future needs for trained leadership in the food service industry and suggests methods for using experience to its greatest advantage. After studying it, the student should:

1. Understand the circumstances that create the industry's need, both today and in the future, for trained leaders.
2. Know the ways in which he can use his experience best.
3. Be capable of using the experience of others, by referral to outside sources.

THE NEED FOR TRAINED LEADERSHIP

The fact that you have enrolled for this formal training indicates that you desire a career in the food service industry. Chapter 1 described the size of the industry and listed many of the choices of career that you will have to find the one best suited for you. A quick look at the employment opportunities in any trade magazine or paper will show that all segments of the industry are looking for trained and qualified leadership now, and this need will continue for some time to come. Because this is such a large and growing industry, you will have an excellent chance to grow with it, which is a most important consideration.

The industry needs not only trained people to lead, but young, aggressive men and women with imagination who are not afraid to innovate and seek new systems and ideas. Many people expound on the multitude of problems and difficulties confronting food service in the future, and in some measure they may be right. No other industry has solved all its problems either, so the food service industry is not unique in this respect. The important thing to remember is that if we had no problems, there would be no demand for new and better management. It is the challenge for needed improvement that has created the demand, and you will become a vital part of this task.

Not only will this career be rewarding in personal achievement and challenge; it also offers good financial rewards. The amount of money you make and the degree of satisfaction you have in doing a good job will be limited only by your efforts. It is safe to say that very few other industries can offer so many opportunities for the future and such fast advancement. As in any profession, formal schooling is a great advantage, but one cannot expect to learn all about anything from books and professors alone. The fact that you will have taken the time and made the effort to learn will indicate to employers that you are interested and dedicated and will open many more doors and opportunities for you. It also shows that you have set a course for yourself, and this too means a lot to any prospective employer, no matter what business he is engaged in.

Many of you have already had some practical experience in food service and will be getting more, even as you attend classes. To some, working part time while going to school will help to pay for your education and provide good experience at the same time. In this respect again, the food industry has an advantage, because there are so many work locations that can fit into your schedules, and a wide selection of working hours—one can work days or nights, or even on weekends, as against the usual 9-to-5, Monday-through-Friday hours in most businesses.

Just as you will strive to get the most from classes and textbooks, you should try to get the most from your practical experience. It is not just the length of time one has spent at something that counts, but what one has learned from this experience. Many people spend years on the same job without ever learning anything new or different. Years ago, it was thought that if you wanted to learn all about something, you should go and talk to the man on the job. For example, to learn the best way to wash dishes, you asked a dishwasher. But when we tried this approach, we quickly learned that most people were doing their jobs the same way they had been taught by other untrained people years before. It was then decided that the best approach would be to make some time and motion studies, do research, and create new and better ways of doing the job.

Certainly, employees come to management from time to time with some very good ideas, but management should initiate and work out the problems and systems. We landed a man on the moon without asking someone who had been there before, and the same approach should be taken in our own research and development. The design and development of items like the convection and microwave ovens did not come from cooks and chefs, but rather from management and equipment manufacturers who recognized a need for some new devices to help with food handling.

GETTING THE MOST FROM EXPERIENCE

Just as you should be concerned about the proper way to scramble and serve an egg, you should also be interested in how to get the most from practical experience. Many call this "on-the-job training," but we will change this for the time being to *on-the-job learning*. You will get a certain amount of training and instruction, but your chief concern should be to learn as much as possible on your own.

Varied Experience

When you are first starting, it would be most beneficial to your later career to vary your experience and jobs as much as possible. This does not imply "job hopping"; but the more different jobs you work at, the better your chance to learn and expand. For example, if you work this summer as a short-order cook, think about taking another type of position next summer—perhaps at the same establishment, but as a waiter, or in receiving and issuing. You might like one job better than another, but you should be thinking in terms of the long haul and your goals for the future.

In addition to taking different jobs, you can also give some thought to exploring the many different parts of our industry. Look for a place that will offer a change of pace from the one where you worked previously. You will learn a great deal. In the hotel school I attended in the thirties, all the students had only one goal—to work at the Waldorf Astoria in New York City, because of the glamor. When the opportunity finally came, it was a shock to find that the Waldorf was not doing well (all hotels had a great deal of operating difficulties) and that the wages were low. I ended up working for a small chain of drive-in restaurants that later became the Marriott

Corporation, now one of the giants. The first chapter listed almost two dozen different branches within the industry, so it should not be difficult to get variety.

Observation

When working on any single job, make a real effort to look about and see what the others are doing in the same department or in others. If you are working in the warewashing section, you can observe what the cooks are doing and how they do it. When it comes time to restock the service stand with clean dishes, study how the servers go about their duties—the manner in which they place their orders—and how these orders are filled and placed into the pickup position. Just because you are engaged in one particular job does not mean you cannot learn something about what the others are doing. This is one of the best ways to pick up some valuable ideas for the future and also to give you an idea of what you would like to try next.

Analysis

At the same time that you are observing what the other employees are doing, observe the entire operation and try to evaluate it. No one is an expert when first starting, but there are certain things that do not take an experienced eye to detect. Think about some of the following obvious things.

Cleanliness of the Facility. Is it clean most of the time, or only at certain times while operating?

Noise and Confusion. Do things run in an orderly fashion, or is there a lot of arguing and bickering among the employees?

Speed of Service. Can the servers get their orders quickly, and are the guests served promptly?

Quality and Appearance of the Food. Naturally, you will get a chance to eat certain prepared items, and from time to time you will get the chance to notice the food being served to customers. Are the dishes attractive? Is the hot food served hot on hot plates, cold food served cold?

Control. Look around and note security provisions. Are doors to storage areas or to the rear exit kept locked, or could someone easily walk away with something? What about portion control? receipt of incoming merchandise? food and materials storage? After a little practice in observing items like this, you will soon be able to tell quickly whether or not a facility has good or poor control.

Productivity. Are all employees working in an orderly fashion, or does there seem to be a lot of needless running and moving about that could be eliminated? The important thing to remember here is that when people are running or walking a lot, they are not producing.

Training. What training procedures are used? Did someone with knowledge show you the best way to do your job, or were you just thrust into it to figure out your own way? Do management and the other key people seem to know what they are doing in the matter of instructing others?

Attitude of Employees. Do they seem happy with their work, or are they disgruntled most of the time? This is something that can be detected in a very short time in any operation.

You do not have to be an expert or have many years of experience to spot obvious conditions like these in food service operations, but many people with long experience fail to notice obvious faults because they are too engrossed in working in the same place day in and day out. Often, someone from the outside can come in and quickly see things that were wrong that the manager had failed to observe.

Early in your career you must train yourself to observe what is going on around you; the ability to note weaknesses and do something to correct the situation is what makes good management. For example, in one restaurant many years ago, the sandwich maker was always behind in filling orders, and at the end of the day she was exhausted. A little observation of her work revealed that the loaves of bread were on a shelf behind her; each time a sandwich was ordered, she had to turn around, take two steps, get the slices of bread, return two steps, and then make the sandwich. The solution was simple: A shelf was installed over her work station so that the bread was in front of her and within easy reach. A large chain operation once installed secret cameras in its kitchens to record work habits. The results were amazing—even a novice viewing the films could detect scores of mistakes being made. It is amazing what a little observing and analysis can detect, and in many instances, the solutions to what seem great obstacles are very simple. Try being your own camera, and note some of these things early in the game so you will be prepared to do the job right in the future.

Possible Improvements

When observing a facility, think constantly of things you would do to correct some of the weaknesses. In the case of an employee bringing cans of fruit from the storeroom, a small, inexpensive cart would reduce the work load; adding that small shelf over the work station helped the sandwich maker; minor changes in equipment arrangements can often improve efficiency; adding more service ware—dishes, glasses, cups, and so on—can prevent servers from running about madly looking for something to serve in. When problems arise, many managers tend to throw up their hands and exclaim that the whole place needs changing from one end to the other. There are instances where this might be true, but more than likely the situation could be improved greatly by a series of small changes and ideas. It is sound practice to do the very best with what exists and then, if troubles are still apparent, consider more major changes.

Very few existing food service operations could not be improved considerably with a series of minor changes and some new ideas and systems. This is what keeps management companies in business; this type of company is called in to run a facility that is in trouble, and it is usually able to make improvements and put the operation back on its feet without large changes and investments.

Good Features

Too many of us, when starting our careers, are preoccupied with all the things that are wrong or need correction. Often, we fail to note some of the plus features almost every food service operation has. This is a most important consideration in building your experience record and making it worthwhile.

Most individual operators over the years have come up with some excellent ideas and systems that are worth noting and copying. It might be a particularly good recipe, an efficient method of food handling, a good control system, or small devices that have been invented to help in the dozens of chores around the place. For example, the Reuben sandwich that has become so popular was developed by an individual facility and entered in a national sandwich contest; the rest is history. Much of the equipment on the market today was developed or refined by people working with it every day. The modern check wheels, tools for holding checks in order so the cook can fill them, developed from a homemade device made from a wire and some wooden clothespins in the beginning. Necessity is the mother of invention, and you are sure to see many new and different ideas during your working tour. Note these at least in the back of your mind for future use. Then, as you run into the many problems of operation in the future, one of these ideas you have seen in the past just might be the answer.

Trade Magazines

No matter how long one has been in the business, it pays to read and scan as many trade magazines and papers as possible. This is an easy and fast way to find out what is going on in the industry—new trends, what others are doing, the results of surveys, new ideas, new equipment. The same thing applies to the many trade and equipment shows; try to attend as many of these as possible, and also to engage in the various panel discussions that can be very informative. Look and listen for new ideas and methods constantly, because this is what will eventually solve the many problems confronting us.

Films

In addition to the numerous training manuals available covering all subjects, there are many fine training films available from different sources, such as the government, processors, manufacturers, and so on. Once again, the important thing to remember is that you might see four or five of these films and not learn anything, but the sixth one might be of tremendous help. The development of top managers in the future will come not from any one school, text, film, or other aid, but from collecting good ideas from a great number of sources. It is the addition and use of these many small improvements (not some fast miracle solution) that will produce important results.

Other Operations

By all means, visit and inspect as many other food operations as you can. Most of us make the mistake of checking only the facilities that are like our own. If we are working in a cafeteria, for instance, we have a tendency to visit just other cafeterias. Instead, try to see a wide variety of operations and find out what they are doing of interest. Earlier in the text, we described how certain methods and systems were taken from one segment to another—adaptations that proved successful. There is still a lot of interchange needed that would help everyone in the business.

The Customer's Viewpoint

When you are eating out somewhere, pick a table or seat where you can see as much of the operation as possible. Note both the good and bad things—the greeting, service, quality and appearance of the food. Note how others around you are doing, listen for comments, check the atmosphere, comfort, cleanliness, and prices. Put yourself in the customer's shoes and you will learn a lot about what the customer expects and wants, which will be of great help to you. One of the large chains once insisted that all managers take their spouses out for dinner once a week at company expense, so that they would have a better customer understanding. Too many of us have become so engrossed in the operation or the back of the house that we have forgotten about the customer, and this can be a serious mistake, because he is the one who pays for everything.

Ask Questions

Too frequently, people think that because they have graduated from college or are in management positions, they are supposed to know everything, so they are hesitant to ask questions for fear of showing ignorance. This is wrong. Not only should you ask *how* a thing is done, ask *why*, which is more interesting and may be harder to answer. So often, people do things day in and day out without ever stopping to find out why.

At one time, a large chain was having trouble with each of the newer units being opened; there seemed to be a "gap" between the people doing the designing and the operations people. It was finally discovered that the planners were hesitant to ask questions of the operators for fear of showing their lack of knowledge, and that the people running the places could not read and understand blueprints but did not want to admit this. Someone was selected to work with both groups and bring them together, a step that proved to be successful.

It is impossible for anyone today in any business to know all there is to know, regardless of intelligence or years of experience. Ask questions early in the game, and keep on asking them throughout your entire career. You can learn a lot more by listening than by talking!

Move Ahead

The name of the game is advancement—moving up to jobs with more responsibility and pay. To be realistic, you must put some effort of your own into this process. Most company personnel handbooks stress the fact that merit advancements and increases will come automatically, based on performance of the individual. There are many times this does happen, but there are just as many times when it does not. If you think you have done a good job and it is time to move up into another position, talk to your supervisor or superior and at least mention the fact. This does not mean you are dissatisfied with the company or your job, but it does mean you have some initiative and ambition. Most companies appreciate this type of employee, because he has shown some drive and interest.

The time may come when you have gone as high as you can with an organization, but you wish to continue even higher. A decision must be made then about transferring to another company or seeking other endeavors. In brief, you must supply a little "push" of your own to your career—advancement doesn't come like bananas falling off a tree.

SUMMARY

1. *Need for Leadership.* The food service industry, because of the changes and improvements that must be made in the future, is in great need of new leaders who not only are trained in the necessary functions, but can bring in the imagination and innovation required to solve the industry's current and anticipated problems.

2. *Value of Experience.* Schooling can be of great value in training new leaders, but the most important possession they can have is a wide variety of experience—"on-the-job learning"—that involves having worked in many kinds of jobs and in many types of places.

3. *Using Experience.* To make the best use of his experience, the student should observe, analyze, use trade sources

of information, ask questions, and check facilities from the customer's point of view. Then he will be in a position to make necessary improvements, and also to advance as fast and as far as his talents will permit.

QUESTIONS FOR REVIEW

1. The last time you ate a meal in a restaurant you were unfamiliar with, did you notice anything regarding the food or service that called for improvement? Thinking back now, after reading this chapter, can you think of anything else that might not have struck you then?

2. Referring to question 1, what were some of the good features of the restaurant? Did you spot any clever innovations being used? any practices that were better than those in other places?

3. List, in two columns, the plus and the minus features of an eating place you visit often. Then, next time you go there, take the list along, check it to see if each item still applies, and add anything you may have omitted. Do you think the manager would be interested in seeing the list?

4

Control

Objectives

As with any business, control—the subject of this chapter—is the central factor in the food service industry. The student who has studied this chapter should be able to:

1. Enumerate the functions and value of financial reports.
2. Understand the reasons for the central importance of control in the food service industry.
3. Describe the areas in which control is essential, and some of the methods of maintaining it in each area.

The most essential factor for success in food and beverage service is complete control. This ingredient is vital for every type of service and operation, whether the goal is dollar profit or the need to stay within a given budget. In the past, control was associated solely with accounting, but we have learned that total control goes far beyond accounting alone, even though the two are related. In fact, one can have a fine accounting system and still not have control of the operation.

FINANCIAL REPORTS

Most standard accounting systems now in use are primarily concerned with two basic reports.

Balance Sheet

A balance sheet can be made out at any time, as often as necessary. Its purpose is to report net worth, or, in simple terms, the difference between the total assets and liabilities, at a given moment. If you have more assets than liabilities, there is a net worth on the plus side; if you owe more than you own, then the venture could be in trouble.

Profit and Loss Statement

This is sometimes referred to as the operating statement. Its purpose is to relate for a given period of time the results of the operation—profit or loss, or deficit or surplus in some cases. Normally it is made out monthly, to cover a calen-

53

dar month, but it could cover various periods of time according to people's desires.

In brief, it will tell you that last month you took in a
certain amount of money, spent a certain amount, and ended
up with either a profit or a loss. With most accounting systems, it takes from one to two weeks to arrive at these results
because of very complicated inventory systems, so that you
might be forced to wait until October 15 to know whether or
not you made money during the month of September.

Although these statements and figures are needed in
all operations for a variety of reasons, it is easy to see that
they are not very helpful in the day-to-day control so neces-

sary now. Granted that they will eventually tell whether the operation has made or lost money, by the time the truth is known, it may be too late to make the needed adjustments. Once the money has been lost in a previous period, there is no way to go back and recoup the loss—and in fact, it can be very difficult to find out just where the loss occurred or determine its cause. What we need is almost a daily—or even hourly— set of figures and controls that will indicate immediately that

TABLE 4-1

A Simplified Profit and Loss Statement

Profit and Loss Statement for Restaurant X

Current Year

Sales:		
Food	$ 600,000	
Beverages	200,000	
Total sales		$ 800,000
Cost of goods sold:		
Food	240,000	
Beverages	60,000	
Total cost of goods sold		300,000
Gross profit		500,000
Expenses:		
Salaries and wages	240,00	
Other expenses[a]	100,000	
Total operating expenses		340,00
Operating profit[b]		$ 160,000

Note: This example covers an entire year; in most operations, a profit and loss statement is made for each month, and then yearly.

[a]Other expenses would include all the other operating expenses involved in the operation—employees' meals, paper goods, laundry, heat, light and power, printing, etc.

[b]Operating profit is profit before taxes and all other fixed expenses, such as rent, depreciation, etc.

something is wrong, so that changes can be made to keep the operation in line at all times. It is like navigating a ship or a plane: You can't just set some controls and wait for hours and days with the hope that it will reach the chosen destination; the position must be constantly checked all through the voyage or flight to make sure that the proper course is being followed. A subsequent chapter on "Forecasting and Guidelines" will go more into detail on what figures and checks we need in the food service industry to keep us on the right course so that those profit and loss statements and balance sheets will come out right.

NEED FOR GOOD CONTROLS

Even though most facilities will insist that they do have control, there are many signs that would dispute this fact. A glance each month or each quarter at the results from even large chains will show wide variations in the profits and losses—one quarter will show a large profit and the next will indicate a loss, all of which means there is a lack of control someplace. A large management company for food service facilities claims that the first thing it does when taking over an operation in trouble is to install effective controls, a procedure that in most cases solves the problem of loss or failure to meet the budget. One widely used textbook for food service management stated that less than 40 percent of the food service operations even bother to check and receive merchandise with any degree of accuracy or consistency. A recent article in one of the trade magazines pointed out the fact that pilferage in our industry has risen to as much as 7.5 percent of the gross sales in some instances. Over the years, the food service industry has been well known for the number of business failures—a much larger percentage than in many other industries. Despite what many may say, *we have not had control, and we still do not have the degree of control that is needed.*

Another factor has entered the picture in recent times. Years ago, we were dealing with very low-cost food, materials, and labor, so we could accept some losses here and there, because they were not serious or too costly. In other words, it was possible to make money despite the lack of control or knowing what we were doing—but that picture has changed and could continue to get worse in the future. Whenever costs rise and profit margins become smaller, it becomes vital to install rigid controls in order to be successful.

Once, the cost of such poor operating practices as these was not large enough to hurt the end results too much:

Some pilferage

Delivery shortages

Food shrinkage

Little or no portion control

Overpouring at the bar

Waste of food, materials, and energy

Low employee productivity

Errors on checks

Omissions on checks

Missing checks

Now, however, we are in a position where these leaks can be really serious, and they must be plugged. When one is losing only 1 percent of gross sales in pilferage, it may not be a serious matter, but when that figure starts to climb to 7.5 percent, it is time for action.

AREAS OF CONTROL

The best way to define the areas of control is to start at the back door and go right through the entire facility and out the front. The important thing to remember is that each of these areas must be under tight control at all times; many of us are very conscious of cash security, for instance, but fail to realize that all the other items, such as food, also bear close watching. We will keep that dollar securely locked in a safe while ten dollars' worth of food is either going out the back door or failing to come in on a delivery. On the profit and loss statement, a dollar's worth of anything—whether it be food, soap, or china—will mean the same as that dollar bill, and this is a very important consideration.

There is another very simple way to illustrate the seriousness of losses, even those that seem minor. For example, say that operation X nets a 10 percent profit. In other words, for every $100 in gross sales, there is $10 dollars in profit. If this is true, then every time $10 dollars is lost through waste, pilferage, or any other reason, operation X must do an additional $100 dollars in gross sales to make up the loss that never should have happened. In brief, if X does not have controls, a lot of people are doing a great deal of work for nothing. The object, as with any business, is profit, and no business can survive too long without it.

Specifications

Everything that is purchased must have some sort of written specification that is followed by the person placing the orders. Specifications can range from very lengthy and detailed descriptions to very simple standards, but in all instances it is essential that some standards be set and followed. Particularly in the case of food, it is difficult enough to maintain quality with highly standardized raw ingredients, but when all grades and sizes are purchased, then the whole operation can be in trouble. Following strict standards, or course, rules out bargain buying, but this has never proved to be a good practice in the food service industry.

For example, a manager has learned from experience or testing that the best rib roast for his purpose is one of Choice quality, averaging very closely to a certain weight for each rib, and oven-ready. His cooks have become accustomed to this and soon learn the proper cooking time and the right carving to produce the number of servings desired. But if a different size and quality rib is purchased the next time, great care must be taken to instruct all the cooks and servers in a new set of cooking and carving methods. If one keeps changing the items each time they are purchased, it is easy to see the confusion and trouble that will result.

This does not mean that specifications can never be changed, but we must realize that everyone handling the product must be instructed and shown how to use the new item. Naturally, there will be times when the product you wish will not be available in the size and quality desired, and something must be substituted. When this happens, management must be sure to notify all the people involved of the change; otherwise there will be problems. There is always that temptation to buy the bargin or something cheaper—even in the rather simple case of hamburger. Normally, ground meat or patties are specified, of a certain quality, with a limit on the amount of fat per pound allowed. By adding more fat than this amount, it would be possible to buy for less, but there would be more shrinkage in the cooking, and the customer would soon notice that the meat portions were smaller. Experience by many successful operations over the years has proved that it is best to set standards for all items purchased and to stick to these standards as closely as possible.

Purchasing

Once the specifications have been developed and set, all purchasing should be done according to these specifications. Years ago, it was common practice to make up a list each day of the items needed, then call two or three dealers for prices on each item. The prices were compared, and certain items were allotted to certain dealers based on the lowest price. But because of the current lack of clerical help and skilled people who can devote enough time each day to such a system, most operations today have certain dealers for certain products. These dealers have been given the specifications and standards and normally are called to supply the needs. This system should not rule out periodic shopping and comparisons—it is not good practice to be "married" to one certain dealer, as the saying goes—but the daily shopping and bargaining routine is a rather difficult road to take.

The other important control on purchasing is that all purchases must be based on sales or needs. Two pieces of information are necessary to facilitate this: One must know what is on hand before placing the order, and also have some idea of the number of items projected to be sold in the future.

Most purchasing is done on a hit-or-miss basis—what someone thinks will be needed, without knowing for sure. This can hurt an operation in one of two ways—being overstocked on some items, resulting in waste and shrinkage, or being out of needed items that are popular on the menu. Beverage purchases should also be closely tied to sales and what is needed, or the same problems could arise.

Just as there are always "bargains" available on certain items, from time to time salesmen will offer special discounts for buying large quantities—50 cases of canned tomatoes at a special price, or large quantities of a slow-selling brand of liquor. You should be wary of this practice, because if you are not set up to handle large quantities of food correctly, or if the "bargain" is a slow mover, the costs of extra handling, breakage, shrinkage, pilferage, and spoilage could soon wipe out the discount you obtained by buying in such large quantities.

A good simple rule to follow in purchasing is to buy only what you need and what you can sell. Large inventories of slow-selling merchandise of any kind will eventually cost an operation much more than they can save. Savings can be made by purchasing wisely, but that does not mean on low price alone.

Receiving

It was mentioned earlier that less than 40 percent of the food service operations receive merchandise correctly; this can be seen readily by visiting and observing many different kinds of facilities. When cash or change is received, great care is always exercised to count and recount to make sure the correct amount was tendered. Yet when shipments of food, beverages, and supplies costing many hundreds of dollars are delivered, someone will quickly sign the delivery ticket without even counting or checking the merchandise. Many operations have no receiving scale, or if they do, it is in a corner and never used. If you are not getting what you are paying for, there can be substantial losses right at the start that will be difficult to overcome.

There are several rules that make for good receiving, and they must be followed diligently:

1. An open area must be provided inside and near the delivery entrance, where all deliveries can be placed to be received and checked.

2. This area must have a scale that is in good working order and in view of the person making the deliveries.

3. All invoices or delivery tickets should be clearly written, indicating the item, description, size, quantity, price, all extensions, and total. If any supplier refuses to furnish such an invoice, it would be better to change to another supplier.

4. Someone in authority must be assigned the task of receiving and be available for each and every delivery. This is a most important function and cannot be neglected.

5. Either the person doing the receiving must know the specifications for all items being checked in, or a brief descriptive set of specifications must be available at all times for reference.

6. Where the weight of an item is the important factor, the item must be checked on the scale to make sure its weight agrees with that on the invoice. If there isn't time to check each and every package, at least spot checks should be made. Even supposedly sealed packages of meats with weights printed on them could be short, so nothing should be taken for granted.

7. Receiving beverages (liquors, etc.) requires special attention. One must make sure of the size of the bottles—if quarts are specified, one could get a case of fifths instead. The cases should be opened to make sure no bottles are missing; it is possible to get a standard table of weights for various sizes and cases, and this too can be done. Again, it is important to check

the labels. If you have specified an 8-year-old scotch of a certain proof, make sure this is what has been delivered.

8. It was stressed above that all invoices should be clearly written, priced, extended, and totaled. At the time of receiving, these figures should be checked, and if there are errors, this is the time to get them corrected. Small adding machines and even pocket calculators are available at low cost, so that this job can be done easily and quickly. If there is an error, note it on the invoice, make the correction, and, if necessary, have the deliveryman call his office to get verification at the time of delivery. This will save much time later.

9. Once the delivery has been checked and found to be in order, the deliveryman should leave the material in the receiving space. Many operations have the deliveryman put the materials on the shelves, etc., in their storage areas, but this is not a good practice. Have someone on your own staff of employees put the merchandise where it belongs.

These precautions may seem like a needless waste of time, but when you think of the value of the merchandise being received and the possibilities for loss, you will see that one can't be too careful in the matter of receiving. Realize that hundreds and thousands of dollars in merchandise is coming in that back door, and that there could be some rather significant losses here. Even if we assume that shortages are unintentional, they still constitute a loss to the operation. And if one has the reputation of not receiving correctly or paying much attention to this function, there could be a lot of intentional shortages as well.

Storage and Security

Once the material has been received, it should be placed in the proper area for bulk storage. New supplies must be stored so the old supplies are used first—a very important consideration, especially with foods. All storage areas should be equipped with secure locks and be controlled. Make every effort to see that these main storage areas are locked and secure most of the time. They should also be off limits except to authorized personnel—they must not be available to deliverymen, salesmen, or just anyone who wants to go into them. If you had, say, $5,000 in cash instead of $5,000 worth of food, liquor, and supplies in these main bulk-storage areas, you

would have the doors securely locked at all times and be very sure that only certain authorized people went in. As far as profits and losses are concerned, $50 worth of merchandise is the same as $50 in cash.

Issuing

Controlled issuing of all supplies is a very desirable feature for any food service operation. However, most smaller operations cannot afford all the clerical help that this would entail. In most cases, the position of issue clerk has vanished from the scene, and if there is any control at all, it must be done as a part of some other position. The old food-control systems were based on the fact that everything from the storeroom had to be on a requisition, and at the end of the day these were priced and extended to give an accurate daily cost of food. Because we are unable to maintain these large staffs now, changes have been made.

Even if one does not issue by formal requisition, it would be wise to have some sort of orderly method for supplying goods from bulk storage areas. The idea of leaving all storage spaces open continuously and having everyone make hundreds of trips in and out as they need a can of this or a jar of that is not only bad for control, but it causes a lot of needless steps and effort that could be avoided. In the search to find out why the food service industry was at the bottom in productivity, one of the main causes was found to be that the average food service worker spent 25 percent of his or her time walking. To get some semblance of control and increase efficiency, open the main storage areas at only certain times of the day. Personnel of each department can make up a list of what they will need on their stations and, with the help of carts and racks, make one or two trips and stock their work areas. Then the main storage areas can be secured until the next issue period.

Years ago, one of the major restaurant chains insisted that their main storeroom be placed near the dining room because the servers had to make so many trips to and from the storeroom as they needed various items. It is difficult to imagine how one can take care of customers' needs in the dining room when one must spend so much time running back and forth to the storeroom. Regardless of the size of the facility or the number of employees, some sort of control and security can be established for the storage of food, beverages, and other supplies.

Menus and Merchandising

The menu is the key to the control problem for all types of food service. The menu must fit all parts of the facility—the market, the layout, the equipment, the skill of the employees, speed of service, storage facilities—in brief, this is the guiding factor for success. Not enough attention and effort is given to the menu in most instances, and this could cause a lot of difficulty and unnecessary expense.

The main problem with most menus is that too many items are being offered at one time. The feeling seems to be that the more items offered, the better the acceptance by the consumer, but this is not true. It is the quality of the food and service that makes the difference, as has been proved by the many successful operations working with limited menus. The more items one is forced to buy, store, prepare, and serve, the more difficult the control problem. A careful study of sales records will reveal that many items are being handled that could be eliminated to save a great deal of work, effort, and loss.

Preparation

Food preparation is another prime control area overlooked by many. This, too, works both ways—if too much food is prepared, there will be a loss or waste, and if not enough is prepared, there will be runouts and slow service. Again, a good sales record is needed to forecast just how much should be readied each day, and above all, if the operation is preparing food from scratch, good recipes are a must.

One should not leave the amount of food to be prepared up to the cooks. Management should establish each day from their records the amounts or portions to be prepared, depending on the selection of items and past history of sales. Then, too, more attention is needed in portioning of all items. In many kitchens, it is difficult to even find a portion scale; if there is one, it is usually under a table or up on a shelf, gathering dust. These scales are inexpensive, and each production department should have one to constantly check weights. Many depend only on the eye to determine sizes, and this can be costly.

Food and Beverage Service

After the food is prepared and all serving stations are stocked, we find another area that needs good control. Control of food and beverage service depends mainly on portion control, and every effort must be made to eliminate waste and loss. When food reaches this point, it may already be portioned and ready for service, or it may again need regulation and supervision to make sure the right amounts are being served. Portion control not only makes sure that the establishment is not overserving but also ensures that the consumer is getting what he is paying for. Bar control is also very essential; if 1¼ ounces of liquor is served one time, and 1 ounce or 1½ ounces the next, the customer is certain to notice the variations and be unhappy. This same factor goes all down the line, affecting whatever is served. If I get a generous 3-ounce ladle of dressing on my salad one time and a skimpy 1-ounce ladle the next, I will notice. Good control not only is beneficial to the operation itself, but makes for more satisfied customers.

Of course, control in the service of either drinks or food goes far beyond the size of portions—it also involves the quality of items served, the temperatures at which they are served, the cleanliness of the serving equipment, and many other factors. And time can also be important; many times, one goes to a place and receives fine prompt service, only to go back again and be forced to wait for what seems an eternity to enjoy a meal.

Meal or Cash Control

Just as important as getting what you pay for is getting paid for what you sell. Again, good control systems must be established in advance, whether the operation be self-

service or table service. Errors on checks, omissions, missing checks, or a poorly trained cashier or checker at the end of a self-service line can cost an operation a lot of money and reduce the chances for normal profit or meeting the budget. The effort should be placed on establishing tight control systems at the start, rather than on spending many hours later trying to find who or what caused the leak or error. It is much like the problem of pilferage—if one does not have good security or protective systems, it will become necessary to hire spotters and spend a lot of money trying to catch the thief, when the loss could have been avoided in the first place by eliminating the temptation and possibility.

Employees

It may seem strange to include the subject of employees under control, but we are buying a product here, just as in the case of food or supplies. In other words, you are engaging the services of someone for a certain number of hours for a given amount, and you should expect a certain return for the money spent. If the scheduling of the employees is not carefully done and the work force does not coincide with the sales periods, or if you have some employees who are not productive and do not carry their load, then you are losing money just the same as if you had bought and paid for a quart of scotch and received only a fifth.

Another important factor contributing to the food service industry's low productivity is that we have not in the past measured what our employees are producing—we have very poor standards. (Our later chapter on operational guidelines will go into this in more detail.) For example, we have no figures to tell us now just how many school lunches should be served per employee per hour or day; we have no norms by which to say that a restaurant should product X dollars per year per employee if it is operating correctly. But there are many ways today to make these measurements and produce these figures, and this will be clearly shown later.

Services

Most food service operations today engage outside companies to perform such services as window washing, lawn care, duct cleaning, pest control, advertising, legal services, accounting, and maintenance of equipment. This is a good idea, and these should be used as much as possible so the food service employees can spend most of their time on the primary job, which is the serving of food. However, we must make sure again that we are getting value received for the money spent on these services. Is the window cleaner coming when he is supposed to, and doing a good job? Are the lawn and shrubs being cared for properly? Do we still have bugs and rodents after paying a company to rid us of this problem? Management should have a complete list of all these services and know what the contracts call for; if the windows are to be washed once a week, there should be a check-off list to make sure they are.

There are other areas of control in our business, but this enumeration will clearly show what is meant by the word *control*. It goes far beyond accounting, as you can see. And the fact is that the food service industry now has all the means and technical equipment necessary to effect very good control in all areas. Because we have been plagued for years with leaks and losses, much time and effort has been devoted, with a great deal of success, to finding ways to stop them.

This effort can be compared in some degree to the progress that has been made in preventing fires in our industry. We now have safer and better equipment, exhaust hoods that filter out grease and are self-cleaning, automatic fire-extinguisher systems that go off at the first sign of smoke or fire—and all this preventive care has reduced the number of fires. Similarly, we have developed equipment and methods for achieving better control—preventing thefts, losses, shortages, waste, and all the other things that add up to poor control and low profits. In short, we have learned how to prevent these mistakes rather than merely compensate for them afterward. It is the old theory of locking the barn door before, not after, the horse is stolen.

As in the field of medicine, more effort is now being put into prevention than cure, and this is the lesson to learn in the field of control. It is simply another facet of the fact that management must know what is going on, as well as what has happened. In fact, if we know more about what is happening, what has happened would have turned out much better. We can expand on this by studying what will happen in the future, a topic we will cover in the chapter on forecasting.

The old saying about an ounce of prevention certainly

holds true in our business. Let's stop the leaks and losses before they happen!

SUMMARY

1. *Financial Reports*. Accounting systems use several types of financial statements, but the basic ones are the balance sheet, which lists assets versus liabilities as of a given moment, and the profit and loss statement, which reports income and expenditures during a certain period of time and shows whether money was made or lost. Both these statements are helpful, but continuous control is necessary if adjustments are to be made in time.

2. *Why Control Is Needed*. The importance of control in any business is, in brief, to make or increase profits. The more direct reasons, especially in the food service industry, are the possibilities of waste, theft and pilferage, overfeeding and overpouring, shrinkage, low productivity, and other problems that lead to loss.

3. *Where Control Must Be Exercised*. A food service facility must have good control systems in all areas in order to be profitable: purchasing, receiving and issuing, security, menu, preparation and service, cash, outside services, and labor productivity. With good controls, much money can be saved—but it must be remembered that losses can occur through spending too little as well as too much.

4. *Loss Prevention*. The industry now has available all the necessary means for setting up control systems to prevent the occurrence of the leaks that have caused so much trouble in the past. All that is required is that management take advantage of this availability, and use the equipment and methods that are at hand.

QUESTIONS FOR REVIEW

1. Name the two most basic types of financial reports, and differentiate between them.

2. What are some of the risks run by a food service facility that does not have a good control system?

3. Assume that you are in charge of purchasing for a large restaurant. Your customary specifications for turkeys include the fact that they must weigh between 18 and 20 pounds each. One week, your resources tell you that the only turkeys available are 24-pounders. What are your alternatives for action?

4. What is described in this chapter as "the key to the control problem"? Why?

5

Merchandising

Objectives

As with any business, the food service industry must engage in merchandising in order to sell its product. When he completes this chapter, the student should:

1. Know the requirements a food service facility must fulfill before promotion takes place.
2. Have a general idea of the types of merchandising that can be used both on and off the premises.
3. Understand what constitutes a proper menu.

The food service industry's primary objective is selling a product, so it must use a certain amount of promotion or advertising to do this. Although it contains large wholesale segments, most of our industry is involved in the retail end, and much of our selling is done in direct contact with the consumer.

Up to a few years ago, most of the advertising was done on the local level, but now we have many nationwide chains that engage in large and expensive national programs to promote and sell food. The scale and amount of this promotion, naturally, depends on the size of the business and the gross volume, plus the extent of the market to be reached.

Large automobile manufacturers, cosmetic companies, oil companies, and others dealing nationally with almost the same product and the same customers have compiled statistics over the years that tell them exactly where to spend their money for the maximum good. But because of our industry is made up of so many individual operations, offers so many types of service, and deals with such a wide variety of customers, it has been difficult to set up good standards regarding the best medium or method for spending the advertising dollar to get maximum benefits. In fact, many successful food service operations do not spend any money at all on promotion and never have; their success has been built up over the years on word-of-mouth advertising—one satisfied customer telling another.

PRE-MERCHANDISING REQUIREMENTS

Before engaging in any type of promotion, you must be sure that what you are trying to promote is good and will be acceptable to the public. Ask yourself the following questions before thinking about spending any money in an effort to get more business:

1. Is my place of business attractive and clean on the outside? Is it inviting?

2. Do I have an appropriate sign that is easily seen and identifies the place quickly?

3. Is the entrance clean and inviting, or will the customers be turned off the moment they enter?

4. Are all the public areas—lobby, rest rooms, dining areas—attractive and comfortable? How about the temperature? drafts? glare? lighting? noise level?

5. Is my food good? *Consistently* good?

6. What about service? Is it prompt and pleasing?

7. Are all the dishes served attractively and at the correct temperatures?

8. What about the prices? Do they fit the place, the items being served, and—what is more important— the clientele?

In brief, the first step in any merchandising program is to take a hard, honest look at what you are doing; make sure you are doing a good job in every respect before trying to lure new customers and increase the volume.

One other point that must be checked is whether, when you do get more business, you can handle it. This has caused one of the biggest snags in our industry on many occasions—the "grand opening" bit, or the big "two-for-one" idea. The big grand opening has been the downfall of many new ventures. After the owner has spent many thousands of dollars and years planning and getting a place ready to open, he cannot wait until the cash register starts to ring and the money rolls in. Often, he won't even wait until the place is completely finished, so the equipment hasn't been thoroughly tested, and the employees are mostly new and do not know what they are doing or where to find anything. To bring hundreds or thousands of potential customers into a mess like this with a huge opening-day extravaganza is sure to be a disaster in the long run. Both the food and the service on that first day may be so bad that most of the customers will never return—in fact, they will tell others to stay away, so all is lost. It takes a well-trained crew several days or more to become accustomed to working in a new operation; how can we expect unskilled employees to immediately start producing on such a large scale? The best solution to opening a new place is to wait until the building and equipment are complete, the equipment has been tested, and a certain amount of time has been spent in training the new employees; then open quietly on what you think will be your slowest meal and day. Perhaps you will have only a handful of customers for the first few days, but at least you can serve these people well and please them. At the same time, your employees are learning their jobs and becoming more efficient.

There are many examples of new ventures that open in this manner and never do get around to the huge expense of the "grand opening"—they do such a good job from the start that the business keeps increasing. However, if you insist on a "grand opening," have one several weeks after the actual opening, so that you will be able to properly take care of all those customers that come in.

In other words, before you do anything in the promotion line, be absolutely sure that you can produce and that you can please the consumer. All of us have read about "specials" in the paper, gone down to the establishment, and found that they were out of the item; in most cases, we do not return. Promises that cannot be filled will do more harm than good and will lose business.

After initial planning, promotion and merchandising in our industry can be broken down into two classifications: on-premises and off-premises.

ON-PREMISES MERCHANDISING

The first and most effective on-premises promotion will be word of mouth, or what your customers tell others. If you are doing an excellent job, this form of advertising will bring in a lot of new customers; if you are doing a bad job of food serving, no amount of gimmicks or promotions will help.

Food and Beverage Displays

Once we have the customer in the house, every effort should be made to sell, and in our business pleasing the eye will sometimes do more to sell than pleasing the taste. This means attractive displays in lobbies and foyers of both food and wine, and display carts of desserts—often, in fact, just seeing an attractive dish served to someone else will prompt the customer to order the same thing. Show off your food as much as possible, but make sure it is attractive.

Buffets

This method of service is gaining in popularity each day, and both the industry and the customers are finding it beneficial. It speeds service, requires less help, and is an excellent way to merchandise and sell food. If the food is well prepared, attractively garnished, and nicely displayed, it is possible to sell many items that people would never think of ordering from a menu.

Like anything else, the success and acceptance of buffet service will depend largely on how well it is done. Just setting up a few tables covered with cloths and putting out unattractive platters of sliced leftover meats, some wilted salads, and a few casseroles of lukewarm food does not constitute the modern buffet. The buffet is not a means for disposing of leftovers and is not directed only to those who cannot afford to eat from the menu. The table itself must be very attractive and the food must look appetizing, with cold foods served cold and hot foods hot. Lighting is also an important factor in displaying the food; ample room must be afforded around the table so that long lines and crowding are avoided; restocking and replenishing must be constant to avoid the look of empty containers.

If you travel around, you will see some very fine efforts in this direction—fine hotels, for instance, that set up lovely buffets each night, employing different themes to please their guests. In a certain very large resort hotel, the gross food sales exceed $2 million a year, and 75 percent of that amount comes from excellent buffet that is operated for almost twelve hours a day. Considering the number of seats they have in relation to the number of guests they feed, they could never achieve their sales figure without this buffet service.

Self-Service Lines

Even in the institutional field, if more care and attention were paid to the arrangement and presentation of the food on the serving line, more food would be sold. In the school lunch program, they are making a big effort to dress up the serving lines and promote the foods that the children should have; a child will be attracted to something that "looks pretty," and the same thing applies to adults. Many of us forget we are in the business of selling food, and too much of the food we are serving today looks as though it has been served before.

Direct Selling

This is one of the best weapons we have in the battle for increased business and profits. Most of our employees have never been trained to sell—the next time you go out to eat, please take note of this fact. Too often, you are shown to a table without even a word of greeting, menus are handed out, and someone approaches the table to take the order, again without any comment. Many times, the customer must ask if the establishment sells drinks or wine, because there has been no indication that they are available. Then when we hear things like, "Do you want soup or something?" "Do you want your coffee with your meal or later?" "Does anyone want dessert?"—is it any wonder that we are not selling food and drinks? Change the questions above to a more positive approach, and the sales would increase quite a bit:

"We serve the finest martini in town!"

"Our French onion soup is delicious!"

"Would you like some wine with your dinner?"

"You'll enjoy our creme de menthe parfait!"

A good example of merchandising can be found in the new trend toward selling bulk wines in many operations. We have tried for years to sell fancy imported wines to the American public, without much success. Not only was the public confused by all the foreign names, vintage years, what wines went with what foods, and the number of glasses in the various-sized bottles, but even the servers were not sure of the facts and of how the wines should be served.

Not too long ago, bulk wines began to be served by the glass, half decanter, or full decanter—with the number of glasses in the decanters explained by the servers; instead of the foreign names and vintage years, the wines were designated in the simplest terms as red, white, or pink (rosé). In almost every case where this new merchandising technique was tried, the sales of wine increased considerably. The lesson learned was that the American public does like wine and will buy it, given the proper approach.

The program is easy to install (see the accompanying illustration), the service is fast, it is easy to explain to both customers and servers, and we can merchandise an item formerly considered to be expensive at a much more down-to-earth price. Several companies are now producing these refrigerated display casks or barrels that can be placed right in the dining areas. Not only are they decorative; they also provide display merchandising to encourage sales.

We must learn to appeal to all the senses in selling food—the eye, the taste buds, the nose, and finally, the ear. All are very important and can do much to increase the check

Advertisement for a Bulk-Wine Service

This is all you need for bulk wine service. Two refrigerated casks for white wine and rosé, and one non-refrigerated cask for red wine. Some restaurant owners prefer a refrigerated cask for red wine since this slows down the oxidation rate and helps preserve the wine.

WINE PROFIT PROGRAM
Choose the price that suits your needs

Buy your wine in large sizes. Almost any wine can be purchased in 1/2 gallon or gallon jugs. This is the most economical way to buy wine.

Serve your customer exactly what he needs—no more, no less. This eliminates the need for odd size bottles and reduces waste. It also encourages wine tasting—a customer who might be reluctant to buy a full bottle won't hesitate to buy a glass of wine.

Speed up wine service—no need to hunt in a dark cellar for a certain brand or bottle. You have the wine on tap at all times, as easy to serve as a glass of water.

Size	Cost*	Selling Price	Profit Per Glass	Profit Per Gallon
4 oz. serving	$.15	$.25	$.10	$3.20
(6 oz. glass)		.30	.15	4.80
		.35	.20	6.40
		.40	.25	8.00
5 oz. serving	.19	.35	.16	4.00
(7-8 oz. glass)		.40	.21	5.25
		.45	.26	6.50
		.50	.31	7.75
6 oz. serving	.23	.40	.17	3.57
(7-9 oz. glass)		.45	.22	4.62
		.50	.27	5.67
		.55	.32	6.72
		.60	.37	7.77

Based on an average cost of $14.50 per case of half gallons (3 gal.)

The Cooler-Cask is a permanent point-of-purchase display. It adds to the decor of your restaurant and suggests the tradition and quality of the wine you are serving.

Best of all, serving wine by the glass is the most profitable way to sell wine. You can tailor the profit structure to your particular needs. The charts to the right show how you can increase your profits with the Cooler-Cask wine program.

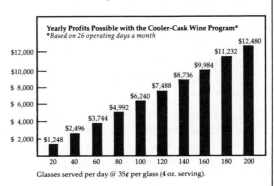

Yearly Profits Possible with the Cooler-Cask Wine Program*
Based on 26 operating days a month

Glasses served per day @ 35¢ per glass (4 oz. serving).

Source: Thomas A. Schutz Co., Morton Grove, Ill.

averages. In fact, with some of the new control systems available today, it is possible to find out which servers are doing a good job of selling by comparing check averages. Teaching your people will take some time, but the effort is well worth while and is a very inexpensive way for the facility to increase business.

Tent Cards and Clip-ons

These can also be used to boost the sales of certain items effectively. However, they can be overdone, and when this happens, the results are not helpful. More than one tent card on a table at any one time just adds confusion and clutter, but one very well done card can boost sales of an item. It is also a good idea to change the cards from time to time, promoting another food, wine, or beverage, because when the customer sees the same card on the table week after week, it loses its appeal. Clip-on specials attached to the menu also do a good job, unless they are overdone—as in many places, where the entire menu seems to be covered with clip-ons. This is defeating the purpose. A clip-on is designed to sell a special item—something a little extra, or at a reduced price—and if the entire menu is covered with them, the place becomes a bargain basement.

Menus

The subject of menus can be most perplexing, because there are almost as many different ones in the industry as there are establishments or chains. Experience shows also that seldom will any two people in the food service industry agree on the subject.

The variety of what we call menus can include handwritten sheets of paper; mimeographs; beautiful, elaborate, and expensive cartes printed in many colors; blackboards; lists written on wood planks; and so on. Wine and beverage lists can vary from a simple tent card to something that looks like a book, with as many as 30 or 40 pages. Some restaurants have no printed or written menus at all; one of the most successful in the country, in fact, sells the same four entrees each night, and they are listed on a small sign over a cashier's booth where the guest pays in advance.

Many books have been written and are available on the subject of menus. Most of them disagree in every particular—the size, number of pages, terminology, number of items, location for various items, pricing, descriptions, and practically everything else. Many years ago, most menus were very similar—they were large, carried many items, were quite elaborate, and used mostly foreign-language terms. The main idea then was to impress the customer with the menu; the fact that it was written in French, for example, would lend prestige to the establishment even though it confused the customer. There are some gourmet restaurants still in operation that do this, and there will probably always be a market for it.

Instead of stating, "This is the way a menu should be written," or, "The best menu is this," let's look at a general list of suggestions and ideas regarding menus. Many still think a menu is not elegant unless it has a silk cord and a tassel, or not effective unless it is about the size of a picket sign. No one can actually say who is right or wrong, but we have learned some basic facts over the years regarding menus.

Clean. Next to being seated at a table full of dirty dishes, glasses, and silver, being handed a dirty, spotted, worn, and frayed menu is about the poorest way to start a meal. However, this is by far the most common fault to be found with menus in our industry. We all know that cleanliness is a must in our business, and yet many places present the guest with a menu that looks as though it has been in use for years. The management of one large chain once became so frustrated in the attempt to get the managers of the units to discard soiled menus that they changed from a very elaborate menu to a simple one that was printed fresh for each meal. Many places now print their breakfast menu on the paper placemat. This is another way to ensure that the guest will get a clean menu, because a clean placemat must be used for each customer. In addition, the minute the guest is seated, the menu is right in front of him and he can quickly make choices. Someone once said that the two most important parts of any meal are the start and the finish; if these are fine, then chances are the guest will be pleased.

Legible. This means that menus should be easy to read. The type selected should be attractive and easy to decipher; it should be of sufficient size so that most people, including the elderly or those with glasses, can read it with ease. In many cases, we try to put too many items on the menu and then load it down with a lot of lengthy descriptions, resulting in a confusion of small print crowded together so no one can read it. Then we compound this problem by using low-level lighting or a small candle on the table, and the guest would need a miner's helmet with a light on it to read the menu.

Limited. Very few ideas have been of as much help and value to our industry as "limited menus." There are still those among us who disagree with this, mainly because they have never tried it or actually seen what advantages can be gained. These operators still believe that the more items you have on the menu, the more business you will do. But actually, it usually works in reverse.

First of all, if you had 100 entrees on a dinner menu, there would still be guests who would ask for something else. From people in the business who have made very good menu sales counts, and a series of menu surveys made by trade magazines and other organizations, we have learned which items are the most popular, and this is the basis for limiting the menu. Some years ago, a large chain determined by computer that despite the fact that each of their units carried more than 500 food items, 90 percent of their total sales were based on less than 50 items. Besides, the fewer items you must handle, the easier it will be for all departments, with less to buy, store, issue, prepare, serve, account for, waste, and so on.

One last point: *Limited* does not mean no choice or change. In fact, many restaurants serve a limited number of items each day but change items from day to day. And customers appreciate seeing something different once in a while. If you have a billboard-size menu with hundreds of items that never change, it can become more tiresome than the well-balanced limited menu that can be changed.

Organized. Try to set up the menu so the customer can find what he or she wants quickly without reading the entire menu. Most of us start reading anything at the top left, so cocktails and appetizers would be best in this position. Then try to group all the categories in an easy-to-find manner—

appetizers, sandwiches, salads, entrees, desserts, beverages, and so on. For example, in a seafood restaurant I have visited, the menu is grouped by the type of seafood—crab, shrimp, oysters—which sounds logical, but to select an appetizer, one must check each of the many categories. Crabmeat cocktail was under the crab section, shrimp cocktail under the shrimp section, oyster cocktail under the oyster section. This is a very confusing menu and makes it difficult to find items.

It is not hard to plan a well-organized menu. If you have doubts, show some of your guests or employees the new proof and get their reactions.

Language of the Customer. We mentioned earlier the problems of menus in French, and of the difficulty over the years of selling imported wines to Americans who do not understand the foreign names and designations. Quite a few restaurants today are having success in selling "red, white, or pink" wines by the glass or carafe, because the average American can understand this. But many are still using foreign terms for the various foods on their menus. Now, there is nothing wrong with this if both the customers and the servers understand what the terms mean. But there is no doubt in my mind that if we had called vichyssoise by what it really is— creamy potato and leek soup—it would have sold much better in this country.

Very few of the average American people who eat out are linguists or gourmets, or belong to the jet set, so why use terms that they do not understand? In fact, many people are embarrassed to ask what a foreign term means and will pass on to something that they do understand; or if they do ask, more than likely the server will not know either, so the entire transaction turns into a farce. Of course, if you do have an elegant group of customers, then by all means use the terms they understand. What I am saying is, fit the language on your menu to your customer and also to your servers.

Sensible Descriptions. As with hula hoops and zoot suits, we in the food service industry go through our "fad" eras. Quite a few years ago, it was the lengthy descriptive menu that was supposed to sell the item: "A mouthwatering

100% U.S. Choice Ground Sirloin broiled to your taste and served on a delicate butter-grilled roll with crisp green lettuce, red ripe tomato slices, slice of sweet onion, and crisp crunchy pickle." In other words, what we now call a "hamburger with everything." Some description is good, but it can be overdone. Why must we say "red ripe tomato," or "crisp green lettuce"? Who would serve a slice of hard green tomato, or old brown wilted lettuce leaves? Use whatever descriptions are necessary, but limit this as much as possible, If you show beautiful colored photos, the dish may come out looking like something entirely different. When the usual baked potato being offered by most places today is cold and shriveled, in a suit of shiny foil, with an interior that looks like concrete, it would be better to list it as a baked potato rather than a "delicious fresh-baked fluffy Idaho potato"; that description should get you arrested for false advertising.

Easy to Change. Even the most carefully planned menus must be changed from time to time—prices changed, some items dropped, others added for a variety of reasons. If a menu is hard to change, there will be a temptation to mark out items with a pencil or pen, write in items, or, worst of all, scratch out the old price and write in the new. This practice is almost as bad as the dirty menu. A good rule to follow is that if there are only one or two minor changes, the menu should not be marked, but the servers should be instructed to explain the changes. If a number of changes are needed, then print a new menu. Why emphasize the fact that you dropped someone's favorite dish, or upped a price, by marking it with a pen? Like a dirty menu, a marked-up menu immediately gives guests a feeling that the establishment is not professional.

Inexpensive. Like the period of lengthy description, we have also come through the "most expensive menu in town" with tooled-leather backs and silk strings and tassels—some of them costing as much as the meal being served. The basic problem in spending too much for menus is that when you have invested thousands of dollars in them, you are understandably reluctant to discard soiled ones or have them reprinted when changes are needed.

It is a mistake to think something cannot be attractive and in good taste unless it is expensive. I have seen many very attractive menus printed on a single card in one color only. If the type is carefully selected, and items are positioned just right, a menu like this can be most attractive. And as far as the front and back covers of the menu are concerned, many spend far more for the picture on the cover or something on the back than they do for the menu itself, which is what the customer reads. Normally, when the guest is seated, the menu is opened and placed before him, so nine times out of ten, he never even sees the covers, and they could be a waste of money. Make the part that the guest reads look good, and design so that frequent changes can be made without running up a huge bill for menus.

Merchandise. Design your menu to sell the items you want to sell—your specialty, or an item that can be served fast and is profitable. As explained earlier, there are locations on any menu that receive first attention from the reader; this would be the place for that item you wish to feature. Different type faces can be used to emphasize one item over another, or attractive borders used to make something stand out. Sometimes in the listing of the entrees for the day, the ones you prefer to sell can be placed at or near the top, since many people read only until they find an item that appeals to them, rather than studying the entire list. If your main menu doesn't have room for the entire list of drinks and wines, room can often be found in the right spot to at least suggest a cocktail or wine with the meal. This is another reason for having a basic inexpensive menu that can be changed often at minimum expense—it gives you the chance to experiment with various combinations and positions to find just the right arrangement for your particular operation.

Fit the Operation. To serve good food well with prompt service, you must have a menu designed to fit the place. It must match the size and kinds of equipment, their capacity, and also the skill of the personnel. So often, owners and managers see another operation doing well with a certain item and quickly add this to their own menu, without checking to see if their place is equipped to handle and serve it, or whether the help is skilled enough to produce it as a quality dish. If you have one old fryer, it would not be wise to add a lot of fried seafood and fried chicken to your menu; featuring char-broiled food without proper char-broilers will present a problem for the cooks and servers. The better matched your menu, your physical setup, and the skill of your employees, the better your food and service will be.

OFF-PREMISES MERCHANDISING

When you have done just about all that is possible at the location and are still in need of more business and customers, or feel that the operation can handle more, then it is time to seek help from the outside. But, before starting any campaigns, remember to make sure that you are indeed doing a fine job with the food and service, and that you can handle the increased business and hold the new guests that will be coming.

Advertising is a very difficult business in itself, but there are several basic things to remember. When you are ready to launch a campaign, go to someone who knows and understands advertising. In addition to explaining what you want to do, state the amount of money that you can budget for the campaign, whatever it is to be. Then the agency will be in a position to suggest the best medium to give the most effective results for the price.

Usually, advertising works better on a repetitive basis than on a one-time big splurge. It is the continual repetition of a name or product that eventually does the job. This is one of the advantages to being a franchisee with any of the major chains—part of the frenchise fee from all units is spent each year to keep the name of the product and company continually in front of the public.

The agency can match the most effective medium to your type of customer. Decisions must be made about whether to go to newspapers, radio, TV, billboards, specials, or a wide range of possibilities today. Some have even used direct mail, or sent literature to office buildings to induce workers to come for lunch each day. Whatever medium you use will be governed by many factors, but it would be best to seek professional help in this field and to spend only the amount that you can afford to budget.

Again, before you do anything, first make sure you have something worthwhile to sell—otherwise, you will be wasting a lot of money and effort on everyone's part for nothing. Just saying something like "Steaks and Chops" or "Under New Management" will not bring the crowds—the public knows that the new management may not be as good as the old!

SUMMARY

1. *Pre-merchandising Decisions.* Before investing any money in promotion, management must determine whether the facility (a) can please the public it will try to attract, and (b) can handle the additional business the promotion may bring. If there is doubt on either score, changes must be made before promotion is undertaken.

2. *Promotion on the Premises.* Selling to the customer who is already present can be accomplished by means of displays, attractiveness of buffet and self-service items, direct selling by servers and others, tent cards on the tables, and particularly by the use of well-thought-out menus. Menus must be clean, well organized, and easy to read; their elegance or expensiveness is, at best, secondary.

3. *Advertising.* Off-premises merchandising should be handled by professionals. Because of their knowledge and experience, they are in the best position to suggest the medium and the methods that will fit in with your budget to give you the maximum return for your money.

QUESTIONS FOR REVIEW

1. Before undertaking a merchandising program, what should you determine about your present facility?

2. What kind of instructions should be given to servers regarding direct selling of food and beverages in a table-service facility? in a buffet-type operation?

3. Block out a sample menu for a medium-priced restaurant. You need not list all items to be served, but concentrate on placement of categories of food and beverages—appetizers, entrees, wines, etc.—and indicate the number of items in each, approximate size of type, and method of printing.

4. For class discussion: Bring in advertisements, from newspapers or other media, of eating places in your locality, and show what you think is good or bad about each.

6

Buying, Storing, and Handling

Objectives

The physical movement and storage of food service materials is the subject of this chapter. After reading it, the student should know:

1. The reasons for the necessity of firm specifications in in the food service industry.
2. The fundamentals of purchasing in regard to frequency and quantities in ordering.
3. The basic problems involved in storing and handling materials.

At this point in the text, we will take some time to digress a bit.

The purpose of this introductory course is to teach the basics and fundamentals of the industry. An advanced course would go into more of the mechanics and details, but it is most important that you understand why certain functions are important and how they all relate and combine to make for a successful venture.

One of the biggest problems in the food service industry has been a lack of ability to look at the entire picture. In brief, we must learn to get first things first. It is not enough to tell people that they must do various things; we must explain *why*—that is, the relationships of all the duties and tasks to each other. *Why* should you keep accurate sales counts, when many do not? *Why* should more effort be put into food service than into preparation? *Why* all the emphasis on security? *Why* bother to check in goods carefully?

We all know these fundamentals, and many will say that they are "old hat"; but the questions is, if we do know all these things, why don't more in the industry apply them and become more successful? Why does the food service industry have the lowest productivity, one of the highest rates of failure, a very high labor turnover? What is making the jobs of top and middle management so tough, a fact that is evidenced by the difficulty of filling these positions?

Certainly by this time, the food service industry should have solved most of its problems. Actually, it has; the difficulty is in getting the information out to all the thousands of operations, managers, and owners and, more important, seeing that they understand the basics and follow the important rules of the game. This point can best be illustrated by an actual experience.

Years ago, one of the large chains was having a problem with its units. Even though all were very much alike, used the same menus, and had the same prices, there were wide differences between the areas and between the individual units in costs, sales, quality, service, and so on. Someone finally decided it was time to take a close look at the individual management and supervision, rather than spending so much time training waitresses and bus boys. To some, this seemed like a waste of time; after all, when a person becomes a manager of a unit or a supervisor of a group, it is assumed that he or she knows all about the job and what to do. However, the study started first by having everyone in management and supervision submit an hour-by-hour and day-by-day schedule of what he was doing. When this information was compiled and studied, it did not take long to realize that no two were doing the same things. Each had his own idea of what was important—some were spending most of their time in the office; others were talking for hours with salesmen; those who had a cooking background spent most of their time in the kitchen and rarely knew what was going on out front; one purposely kept the number of servers low so he could step in during the rush hours and earn some extra money in tips for himself. In other words, although each was doing what he or she thought to be most important, there was a general lack of understanding of the whole operation and of what was actually important for them to do. Few were out front watching and directing the service during the rush periods, which is exactly where management should be in any food service operation. To make a long story short, the job of management was evaluated, and after some time spent in training and explaining, they all had a better understanding of the job and what was needed.

It is important to realize early in the game that most of the problems can be traced directly to management. One of the basic difficulties uncovered by this study is that management in the food service industry can come up through various departments and therefore have varying interests and views about what is or is not important. A manager who has had a great deal of food-preparation experience may devote most of his time to this; another, with considerable experience in serving, may spend too much time cleaning tables or interfering with the duties of the hostess; one who enjoys purchasing may devote most of the day to this. We all like to do the things we are used to, and oppose learning something new. However, when you reach the management level, it is time to realize that *all* the functions are important, and that they must be correlated if the venture is to be a success.

Earlier in the book, it was explained that the basic fundamentals of operation are the same for all types of food service. We must learn what they are and, what is more important, use the knowledge and information we have to plot the best course. We too must learn the odds and percentages of success for various management techniques, and use them to our advantage.

Nothing can illustrate this better than the subject of buying foods and materials for use in our industry. Many different ideas prevail about what makes for a good purchasing agent, or how to buy, as you will learn from experience. Then, too, there are many questions that arise concerning the way food is bought. Let's try to explain the misunderstandings and why we do certain things, using a few examples along the way.

SPECIFICATIONS AND QUALITY

In many instances, food service operations are paying more for food than it would cost at the supermarket. For example, your buyer has contracted for turkeys at so much per pound, and the next week the ad for the local supermarket features turkeys at a lower price. The tomatoes you are getting cost more than the ones you can buy at the local fruit stand, the melons you get also seem to be cheaper elsewhere, and so on down the line for almost every item of food. There are two basic reasons why our industry must at times pay more for its food than the supermarket or the housewife does.

First, we must buy to specification and serve uniform portions and quality, because we are selling a product. If we bought a ten-pound turkey one day, one of 15 pounds the next, and a 20-pounder the next, it would disrupt the cooking and serving. Also, any change in quality would soon be noticed by the customers. In our instructions, we say there must be three ¼-inch slices of tomato on a bacon, lettuce, and tomato sandwich. If we buy ungraded tomatoes of all sizes, how do we control the making of that sandwich? The housewife can buy a size 36 melon one time and a 45 the next, because she is not concerned about portion sizes—her family is not paying money for uniform portions, so if the size varies, there is no problem.

Second, not only do we need uniformity, but we need better quality than the housewife does. If she buys a cheap cut of beef on sale and it turns out to be tough and flavorless, no great damage is done—her family will be right back for the next meal. If we in the business did this, more than likely we would lose customers. The other reason we need higher quality is that our food takes more punishment from the time it is cooked until it is served. At home, the food is cooked and then served immediately, almost direct from the stove. In the industry, we must cook food sometimes hours in advance and hold it for serving. In other words, our food must be of top quality to start with if it is to take this punishment. A good example of this is coffee: One can buy a cheap grade of coffee and brew it, and if it is served quickly, the taste will not be too bad. However, just let that cheap coffee stand on a warming stove for half an hour, cooling down a bit, and you will soon notice that the taste and flavor have changed greatly.

The same thing applies to many other items we purchase. Why do we pay X cents for a glass when we can go to the local variety store and buy one for half the amount? The reason is simple: The glass we use must be heat-treated and have a safety edge, so that we can reduce the amount of breakage and prevent accidents. If that cheap glass at home breaks and pieces get into the food or someone is cut, there

will be no lawsuits or damages to pay. Then, too, we handle many glasses not too gently, so that our glass must be of much better quality and strength. The same thing applies to the china we buy—it is much more costly, and heavier, because it too must take a lot of abuse. The carpet we put down, too, will take more wear in one day than many home carpets do in years.

It is difficult for many purchasers in our business to resist a bargain or a special low price, and this is understandable. However, just as a hitter takes the fourth pitch with a count of 3 and 0 because experience has shown that the odds are better, our industry should learn to stick with the statistics and play the odds. The important thing to learn is that the "as-purchased price" is not necessarily what determines the end cost, and this is where most of the confusion exists. The cost you are concerned with in regard to food is the cost of that plate or portion when it is served. A cheap cut of meat with excess fat and bone can be bought for a lower as-purchased price, but after it is roasted and has stood for a while on the hot-food table, it will have far less yield, so each portion could cost you more than if you had bought higher quality. Hamburger with an excessive amount of fat can be bought for far less than good-quality, fat-controlled meat, but to get the same size broiled hamburger on the roll, it will be necessary to portion the cheaper meat heavier, and here again, you could be ending up with a product that costs more. This same confusion and misunderstanding between the as-purchased cost and the end cost per portion on the plate that is served is the main reason why frozen and convenience foods have been so slow in being accepted by the industry.

Because of lack of actual testing and costing experience, most in our business find it hard to relate the as-purchased price to the portion cost. This is why most still claim that they can do it better and cheaper themselves—a statement that comes not from facts or actual experience, but purely from opinion. Looking at a frozen pie ready for the oven, with the cost so much per portion, you may automatically think about how cheap flour, shortening, and apples are, and reach the conclusion that the pie can be made for less on-premises. The fact missing is the sum of all the other costs involved in making that pie—labor, supervision, depreciation of expensive equipment, waste, spoilage, and so on.

Years ago, I opened some large tollway restaurants for a chain. When the kitchens were designed, they were set up to be serviced from a commissary, but the commissary was never provided, and we were forced to use all frozen, preprepared, pre-portioned, convenience foods, because we had no storage or preparation areas. The rest of the parent chain did all their cooking on-premises, and I was told in advance that the food cost in these tollway restaurants would be excessive because of the high as-purchased prices I was paying. At the end of the first year, however, the net food costs for the tollway restaurants was 13 percent *less* than the food cost for the restaurants doing all their own preparation.

Ordering systems, forms, and the mechanical part of buying have all been worked out in great detail and are easy to obtain. In fact, one can get standard sets of specifications, sizes, and quality that can be most useful. The important things to remember are the basics:

1. Buy to specification; we must have standard materials of high quality.

2. Look at the end cost, not the as-purchased price.

3. Beware of bargains. Business is well organized today, and if one has a quality item to sell, it is difficult to understand why he should be forced to sell it lower than the going market price.

4. Play with the odds in your favor. Some people do win in gambling, but the odds are always in favor of the house, as any professional gambler knows, and if you gamble every day, you are sure to be a loser.

FREQUENCY OF ORDERING

There can be no set rule for any aspect of ordering frequency, because the practices are so different throughout the industry. The frequency could run from several times a day, for those places that are always running out of supplies, to once a year, for the big chain that contracts for certain items on a yearly basis. Over the years, there have been gradual changes in purchasing in our industry, and they have been for the better.

Changes over Time

First, we are not devoting as much time to this task as we did in the past. Many years ago, most in the business were sure that purchasing was the key to profit and success. Owners of even large operations used to spend half of every morning either at the market, personally selecting supplies and looking for bargains, or else on the telephone, calling a number of suppliers and haggling about prices. But gradually we have learned that this time and talent can be put to better use. Certainly purchasing is important, but there are other functions more essential to the success of the operation.

We no longer have or can afford the clerical staffs that would be needed to receive dozens of deliveries each day and keep all these records, and this fact has induced many to cut down on the number of dealers and deliveries.

The cost of deliveries for the supplier is much higher now, and he must pass this on to his customer just as we do. He must now have a "payload" for his profit—he can't afford to drive around a half-loaded truck.

The increased use of more convenience and frozen foods has also decreased the need for so many deliveries. The less fresh, perishable merchandise we use, the less we will need deliveries. Besides, these convenience foods not only have a much longer shelf life, but they take up a lot less shelf space, which means that orders can be placed less often.

More limited menus throughout the industry have also had an effect on cutting deliveries. If we need to carry only 200 items instead of the 500 required years ago, our ordering job is much simpler, and we can store more of the items needed in the same space.

The Fundamentals

As explained earlier, no one can set up exact instructions for the frequency of ordering, but there are some facts that we do know: The fewer the orders, the less time spent on the phone or talking with salesmen, the fewer the dealers, the fewer the deliveries that must be checked and accounted for, and the less paper work, the better, because we just do not have the clerical or management time to waste today—the skilled people we do have are needed now for more important work.

Some will insist that checking in goods is no problem; all that is necessary is to inform the supplier of the exact time you can do it. However, it is difficult for any food service supplier to be at all the stops at 10 A.M. And two hours spent by an owner at the market trying to save a few cents per pound on some tomatoes could cost quite a few dollars by his not being at the operation seeing what is happening.

QUANTITIES

There are many factors to consider in determining quantities of food and supplies to purchase or order. The volume of business, menus, location, methods of preparation and service, availability of supplies and deliveries, and many more considerations must be taken into account to arrive at what is best for a particular operation. As a result, no one magical set of numbers can be predetermined and used by all; but there are some basic rules that should be observed:

1. Logically, the amount ordered must first be based on what is on hand. This may seem like a rather elementary conclusion, but too often orders are placed quickly, without any idea of what is actually on hand, and this can result in overstocking or running out of items when needed.

2. Quantities ordered should also be based on usage and on only what is needed. Accurate sales records, coupled with good projections, can be an excellent guide for determining just how much to order, whether it be food, beverages, or other supplies.

3. All inventories should be kept as low as possible in accordance with needs and operating conditions. Excessive inventories can be costly in a number of ways:

a. Most food, including frozen, will suffer shrinkage if kept too long.

b. Large inventories often lean to increased pilferage—when people see a lot of something, they figure that one less will not be noticed.

c. Large inventories encourage waste—when employees see large supplies of items on hand, they are not as careful in using them.

d. Excessive inventories can be costly in the labor of handling and rehandling, especially if the storage areas are not adequate.

e. Crowded stockrooms and freezers present a problem in inventory and record keeping—and large errors in inventories can make quite a difference in the results on the profit and loss statement.

f. Heavy inventories can tie up for long periods of time a lot of money that could be used to more advantage elsewhere—even if it is only in the bank, earning interest.

Each operation must work out its own best amounts to carry and arrive at the happy medium of having not too much but enough to handle the business, with as few deliveries as possible. This might seem an almost impossible task, but with a little experience and the right records, the problem can be solved. In the advanced course, you will learn about "par stock"—a system by which a company can arrive at the amounts of all major items needed to do a certain amount of business, and order accordingly.

There are some in our business who like to gamble on the buying. They try to guess when an item will go up or down in price and base their purchasing on what they think will happen to the food market or upon what someone has advised. With all the uncertainties involved, this can be a very risky business and is not advisable. What lures a lot of people into this practice is the fact that they hear only about those who

bought the 5,000 pounds of shrimp that went up the next week; the man who bought the huge supply of beef that went down in price a few weeks later never has much to say. In the same vein, it is hard to find anyone who will admit losing money in the stock market—all we ever hear about are those who made money.

From years of practical experience, we know it is wise to turn over the stocks of food quite often, because there can be losses. Even cases of canned food can go bad very quickly. Let the food broker do the gambling on the market, since this is his business and he knows more about it, and let your supplier carry the large quantities. Food service operations should limit themselves to a sensible amount of everything on hand—only what they can handle, use, and need.

STORAGE AND HANDLING

Proper storing and handling of all the materials needed in a food service operation is a very important function, and also a very labor- and time-consuming effort. Special consideration must also be given today to new methods for handling and disposing of trash and garbage. Fortunately, a great deal of study and attention has been given these problems, and there are many new systems and a lot of new equipment to help with this chore:

1. Storage areas are now larger and better located, to reduce the amount of handling, rehandling, and transportating.

2. We have learned more about temperature control of these areas—lower temperatures for storing frozen products, cooling for dry storage to prolong shelf life.

3. New shelving units have been developed for easier cleaning: mobile, so they can be taken out for cleaning or moved about for more efficiency; special dunnage racks, developed for the stacking of case goods to make better use of space; special mobile racks that will also increase storage capacity and make the movement of foods easier; new, lightweight, easy-to-use carts, dollies, and other equipment to lessen most of the back-breaking labor of carrying everything by hand.

Formerly, when cases of canned goods were received, they were opened immediately and the bottles and cans neatly arranged on wooden shelves. Today, we have learned that it is better to keep these items in the cases until needed—they are less apt to be stolen, there is less breakage, more can be stacked in a given area, and they are much easier to inventory.

We have also learned not to compute the amount of storage needed by the square-foot method. It isn't the number of square feet that determines the amount of goods that can be put away, but rather the lineal feet of shelving. One hundred square feet of storeroom arranged as a room 10' x 10' will give only 26 lineal feet of shelving; the same 100 square feet arranged in a room 7' x 14' will yield 31 lineal feet of shelving— almost 20 percent more storage in the same amount of space.

This is what is meant by "modern" food service— taking advantage of all the new ideas, systems, and equipment that have been developed to make the job of food service a lot easier and more profitable.

SUMMARY

1. *Responsibility of Management.* Managers in the food service industry must realize that their primary duty is overall management and supervision, and must not devote too much of their valuable time and talent to narrow aspects of the field. An understanding of the whole picture—all the functions, and the reasons for them—is vital.

2. *Purchasing.* The use of high quality standards in purchasing is central to profitability. Even though such specifications make for higher as-purchased prices, the end costs are generally no higher, and customers are happier. The reason for firm specifications and better quality than the housewife is accustomed to is the harder punishment taken by both food and nonfood items in the industry.

3. *Ordering Frequency and Quantities.* The frequency of ordering, although it varies among segments of the

industry, has decreased overall in recent times, owing to the fact that more orders—and therefore more deliveries—require time, money, and staff that are no longer available. Inventories must be kept as low as is reasonable, because large ones can lead to shrinkage, pilferage, waste, and high costs of handling, record keeping, and tying up of funds.

4. *Storing and Handling.* New systems and equipment today have improved the storage and handling of food service materials, making them easier to store, longer-lasting, and more movable.

QUESTIONS FOR REVIEW

1. Assume that after years of experience as a chef, you have worked your way up to manager of a large food service operation. Where should you be, and what should you be doing, during the dinner hour?

2. Why is the purchase by a restaurant of top-grade meat at premium prices, rather than medium-grade at a lower price, justified?

3. Differentiate between the as-purchased price of a food item and its end cost. What factors can increase the spread between them?

4. Name a few of the circumstances that have changed purchasing habits in the food service industry over the years.

7

Food Preparation

Objectives

The first of the three basic categories in the food service industry is treated here. After completing this chapter, the student should be able to:

1. Name and define the three classifications of the industry.
2. Understand the advantages of reducing food preparation as much as possible, and enumerate several ways to do it.
3. Describe the purposes and methods of production control.

Before getting into the subject of food preparation, let us enumerate and define the three classifications of our industry, so that there will be no confusion.

Food Preparation. This relates to all the work connected with making or preparing the food—cooking, roasting, cleaning and preparing salads and vegetables, making desserts. In a comparison between a restaurant and other retail enterprises, food preparation would parallel the manufacturing of the product to be sold.

Food Service. Once the basic manufacturing or preparation has been accomplished, the food goes into the hands of the food service people. These are the people who do the frying and broiling, dish up the salads and vegetables, and so on, and get the finished product to the servers.

Food Serving. This is the act of finally setting the finished plate before the public—at the table, a cafeteria counter, or a buffet.

SEPARATION OF PREPARATION AND SERVICE

The best way to study and analyze any problem is to first break it down into parts, and then study the various parts. This process has become essential today in the food service industry. Once, only the chef and the manager were of importance—everything rested on them, so the success or failure of the operation depended on the abilities of two people, or, in some cases, only one. Now that the industry has grown so large and is due to increase even more in the future, it is time that we begin to break it down into smaller segments, to ensure better and more profitable operation.

Then, too, these parts of our business have changed. Food preparation is not the prime function now, because we can buy so many foods already prepared; food service and serving have increased in importance, owing to the demands of the paying guest and the need to do more volume business.

By separating these functions, we can better study and improve the total operation. One can have the finest chef in the world, but if the other two parts of the operation are not efficient, all will be lost. The most highly skilled food server (waiter or waitress) can be very ineffective if he or she cannot get the food from the service kitchen. The successful operation in the future must be strong and efficient in all three of these parts.

More and more, we are separating the jobs of preparing and serving food, not only as functions, but even as to area. Food preparation means all the basic cooking and work needed to get food ready for serving—activities like vegetable peeling and cooking, meat cutting, baking, and, of course, the basic job of steam cookery, roasting, and other heavy range work. Food service is now designated as the area where food is finally dished up, ready to be served to the table—or to be picked up, in the case of self-service—and where "short order" cooking is done.

The degree of separation, of course, depends on the type of operation or the size. In very small food service facilities, it is necessary to combine the preparation and serving of the food, especially if only one or two employees are involved, performing both functions almost at the same time and place.

In the past, preparation of the food was considered the big job, requiring the largest area, the most equipment, and the most-skilled and highest-paid help. In fact, so much attention was paid to preparation that little was left for food service. More money was allotted to preparation equipment,

because it is very expensive, so in many cases, little remained
with which to equip the area that did the serving. By the time
very high-priced chefs, cooks, butchers, and bakers were
hired, not much of the payroll budget was left for hiring competent people to do the serving of the food. This is one of the
main reasons the food service industry has about the lowest
productivity of all industries. We are one of very few retail
operations that still attempt to manufacture and sell a product
on the same premises.

REDUCING AMOUNT OF PREPARATION

When labor was plentiful, skilled help was easy to
find, and the rates were low, this dual job of manufacturing
and selling at the same time did not present much of a problem, but as the help shortage became more acute, it became
more difficult to do both. A choice had to be made, either to
keep on trying to process all this food on the premises and
then serve it, or to switch more emphasis to serving the food
and increasing the sales and productivity.

This is what prompted the first large chains years ago
to build and open commissaries, where all the food was prepared ready to serve and delivered to the individual units. It
had become apparent that, for successful operation of a large
chain of restaurants or any other kind of food service, it would
be impossible to find the number of highly skilled people
needed and, what is more, provide all the supervision required to ensure uniform quality and service of food. From
these modest food-processing plants has arisen another huge
part of our industry, which now processes and prepares bil-
lions of dollars worth of food each year for use by all in the
food service industry.

This is the same basic principle of doing business that
has spread to all other branches of retailing—one specializes
in either the manufacturing or the selling of a product, and
this is exactly the course that the food service industry must
take now and in the future. In fact, this separation has already
reached the point where it is possible to operate any type of

food service operation with little or no basic food preparation and processing on premises.

Of course, there are and always will be those who insist that they can do it better and cheaper themselves, but it has been proved over and over that the less time, money, and effort that are put into preparation and the more attention paid to service of food, the better the results will be. Along with the low productivity in most of the facilities, the industry receives more complaints about poor service than about any other single factor.

When the amount of preparation is reduced, the following advantages will result:

1. Food service will improve. More time, skill, and supervision can be allotted to this part of the business, where it belongs.

2. Building space needed can be reduced. Food preparation areas require the lion's share of the total kitchen. In the past, we figured about 60% of the total building for the "back of the house," and about 40% for the front or the sales areas; now this proportion can be reversed, to as low as 35% for the back and 65% for the front, where the money is made.

3. The amount of equipment needed can be reduced. Because preparation equipment is complicated and expensive, anything eliminated here will mean large savings for the entire project.

4. A great number of operating costs can be lowered:

Labor; not only in number of employees, but in skill and rate of pay.

Waste; doing all your own preparation can result in in considerable and expensive losses and waste.

Contamination; the more foods are prepared from scratch, the greater the chance of contamination and spoilage.

Handling; the more foods are received ready for

service, the fewer the items that must be bought and handled on premises.

Storage; the fewer the items purchased, the more can be stored and controlled.

Cleaning; most of the garbage and hard cleaning jobs are in the preparation area, not the service.

Energy; again, the heavy energy usage in water, gas, steam, and electricity is in the preparation of foods.

As the text progresses and gets into more details, many other advantages of doing less preparation will be observed. For example, most of the bad accidents that happen in the preparation of food are due to the knife work and the dangerous machines used in this area. Speeding sales and turnover will increase profits and reduce many other costs in line with the facilities budget.

To give you an idea of the work involved in basic preparation, four recipes are given on pages 114-117: hunters dish, a stew; Italian minestrone, a soup; coffee velvet pie, a dessert; and potatoes au gratin, a vegetable. Operations with controlled preparation have all recipes worked out as illustrated, usually on cards filed in the kitchen ready for use. In the case of some recipes and items, these cards must be pulled and made available for the cooks and preparation people to follow. I have a complete file of recipes in my office, compiled over the years—a total of more than 1,200 cards, which shows that just filing and distributing the recipes can be quite a job itself.

Take a few minutes to examine these recipes and notice the number of individual items needed for each. Note the time elements, especially where some of the preparation must be done a day in advance; note all the various steps to be taken throughout the process; it should be very evident that food preparation, if done right, is a very difficult job. At home, one can, so to speak, throw dishes together—a dash of this or a pinch of that—but proper large-quantity cooking requires great care in measuring and cooking, otherwise a great

Hunters Dish

Lima beans, dried	2	lbs. 10 oz.	5¼	lbs.
Water, cold	1	gal.	2	gal.
Water, boiling	1½	gal.	3	gal.
Salt	6	tbsp.	4	oz.
Spaghetti	3	lbs.	6	lbs.
Water	4	gal.	8	gal.
Salt	6	tbsp.	⅔	cup
Pork, fresh, cubed 1" pieces	12	lbs.	24	lbs.
Fat	3	lbs.	6	lbs.
Onions, sliced ½" slices	2	lbs.	4	lbs.
Celery, sliced ½" slices	2¼	lbs.	4½	lbs.
Mushrooms, fresh, sliced ¼"				
thick	4	lbs.	8	lbs.
Tomatoes, #10 cans	13	lbs.	26	lbs.
Salt	½	cup	1	cup
Black pepper	1	tbsp. 1 tsp.	2	tbsp. 2 tsp.
Yield	100		200	

1 Soak beans overnight in the cold water. Drain.
2 Cook the beans in the boiling salted water and drain.
3 Cook the spaghetti until tender in the amount of boiling water and and salt as directed.
4 Drain and wash with cold water to remove the starch.
5 Brown the pork in ⅓ of the fat.
6 Saute the onions, celery, and mushrooms in remainder of fat and add the tomatoes.
7 Combine with pork, cover and continue cooking slowly until pork is tender.
8 Add the spaghetti, beans, salt, and pepper to pork mixture.
9 Pour into steam table pans and bake 45 minutes.

NOTE: This may be simmered slowly on back of stove and not baked in the oven.

Service: 1—#5 ladle—#11 plate.

Coffee Velvet Pie

Genesee plain gelatin (Red Seal)	3	oz. (9 tbsp.)	6	oz. (18 tbsp.)
Instant Maxwell House Coffee	2	oz. (1 cup)	4	oz. (2 cups)
Cold water	2	cups	1	qt.
Hot milk	3	qt.	1½	gal.
Sugar	1	lb. 3 oz. (2⅔ cups)	2	lbs. 6 oz.
Salt	2	tsp.	1	tbsp. 1 tsp.
Vanilla	3	tbsp.	6	tbsp.
Egg yolks	10½	oz. (1⅓ cups)	1	lb. 6 oz. (2⅔ cups)
Egg whites	1	lb. (2 cups)	2	lbs. (1 qt.)
Sugar	14	oz. (2 cups)	1	lb. 12 oz. (1 qt.)
Heavy cream	2	cups	1	qt.
Yield	9	9" pies	18	9" pies

1 Combine gelatin and instant coffee; add cold water and let stand 5 minutes.
2 Then add hot milk and stir until gelatin is dissolved.
3 Add first amount of sugar, salt, and vanilla. Blend.
4 Beat egg yolks thoroughly; add warm gelatin mixture, stirring well. Chill until slightly thickened.
5 Beat egg whites until foamy throughout. Add remaining sugar gradually and continue beating until mixture stands in soft peaks. Fold in slightly thickened gelatin mixture.
6 Whip cream until thick and shiny but not stiff. Fold into gelatin mixture.
7 Pour 1 qt. filling into each baked pie shell. Chill until firm.
8 Garnish with whipped cream.

Service: Cut pie into 6 portions—#10 plate.

---

amount of waste will result. Then, too, if the dish is a good one, you want to make sure it will come out the same way each time.

Now that you have examined these four recipes, imagine a menu with several other entrees that must be prepared, one or two more soups, several more vegetables, and quite a few more desserts, including several other pies, and you can get a good idea of the amount of work involved when

Italian Minestrone

Lima beans, dry	1 lb. 2 oz.	2¼ lbs.
Navy beans, dry	3 lbs.	6 lbs.
Split peas, dry	1 lb. 6 oz.	2 lbs. 12 oz.
Water, to cover	3 qts.	1½ gal.
Vegetable stock	9 gal.	18 gal.
Spaghetti	1 lb. 2 oz.	2¼ lbs.
Rice or Barley	1 lb. 6 oz.	2 lbs. 12 oz.
Onion, ground	9 oz.	1 lb. 2 oz.
Potato, diced raw	9 lbs.	18 lbs.
Thyme	1 tbsp.	2 tbsp.
Celery, diced fine	1 lb. 2 oz.	2¼ lbs.
Carrots, cut ½" pieces	1 lb.	2 lbs.
Tomatoes	1½ gal.	3 gal.
Oil (Salad)	1½ cups	3 cups
Flour, Pastry	1 lb. 11 oz.	3 lbs. 6 oz.
Salt	To taste	To taste
Yield	10 gal. 2¾ qts.	21 gal. 1½ qts.

1 Wash and pick over the lima and navy beans and split peas.
2 Cover with water and soak overnight.
3 Drain off excess water, and put soaked beans and peas into vegetable stock. Bring to a boil, and cook slowly for about 3 hours.
4 Add spaghetti and rice or barley at end of the first hour of cooking.
5 Add onions, potatoes, thyme, celery, carrots, tomatoes at end of second hour of cooking.
6 Add oil, flour, and salt.

you attempt to make all your own foods on premises from scratch. Consider another point: If you make a quantity of that hunters dish to serve 200 and a mistake is made in the preparation, you have lost a lot of money and time and effort because the dish cannot be served. Had you bought this already prepared and it turned out to be faulty, you could simply take it off the menu and get a credit from your supplier—at least the loss would not be yours.

Ways to Reduce Preparation

Let's look at some ideas and suggestions for reducing the preparation load so that we can spend more time on serving and other more important functions.

Potatoes Au Gratin

Cook potatoes day in advance of use

Cooked potatoes, new or Maine, chopped in ¼"—⅜" pieces.	A.P., 4½ lbs.*	A.P., 13½ lbs.*	A.P., 27 lbs.*
Coffee cream	1 qt.	3 qt.	1½ gal.
Milk	1 cup	3 cups	1½ qt.
Salt	2⅓ tbsp.	2½ oz.	5 oz.
Pepper	½ tsp.	¾ tsp.	1½ tsp.
Grated York State cheese	7 oz.	1 lb. 5 oz.	2 lbs. 10 oz.
Buttered cheese crumbs (see below)	⅔ cup	1⅞ cups	3¾ cups
Yield	1 pan	3 pans	6 pans
	20 orders	60 orders	120 orders

Oven temperature—350° F.

1 Cook unpeeled potatoes. Cool to room temperature and place unpeeled potatoes in refrigerator overnight.

2 Peel potatoes and carefully chop in ¼"—⅜" pieces.

3 Place cream and milk in a steam jacket kettle and heat. Add chopped potatoes, salt and pepper. Stir until the potatoes are well combined with hot cream mixture.

4 Cook at medium heat until potatoes, cream, milk, and seasoning are well combined and thoroughly heated—the liquid should be partially absorbed and the mixture should be a creamy consistancy.

5 Gradually add grated York State cheese, stirring continuously so the cheese will be well combined with potatoes and cream mixture. Continue to cook at medium heat until cheese is melted.

6 Remove from steam jacket kettle, pouring 2¾ qts. of potato mixture into each buttered steam table pan, and sprinkle ⅔ cup of buttered cheese crumbs evenly on top of each pan.

7 Place in a 350° F. oven until potatoes are heated through and crumbs are a golden brown, approximately 15—25 minutes. Remove from oven. Length of time in oven will depend on how hot mixture is when put into oven.

Fine bread crumbs, sifted	7 tbsp.	1¼ cups	2½ cups
Grated York State cheese	2 tbsp.	6 tbsp.	3 oz.
Butter, melted	1 tbsp.	3 tbsp.	3 oz.
Yield	⅔ cup	1⅞ cups	3¾ cups
	1 pan	3 pans	6 pans

1 Melt the butter and add sifted dry bread crumbs. Stir until crumbs are mixed with butter. Add grated York State cheese to crumbs, stir until cheese is evenly distributed with crumbs.

Note: Do *not* use Idaho-type potatoes for this recipe.
Service: ½ cup (4 oz.)
*A.P.=as purchased.

Balanced Menus. We all know about balancing menus in terms of color, entrees, vegetables, taste, texture, and so on, but it is also possible to balance the work load in any facility by carefully selecting the various items for the day. A little study will show that certain food items require much more preparation than others, and that some very popular items take little or no advance work. When preparing the menu for the day or meal, recognize this fact and select items that will balance your work load. Two or three difficult entrees, vegetables, or desserts on the same meal will make it difficult for your prep area to get ready in time—in fact, some extra help will have to be added in this case. Because of the shortage of both skilled and unskilled help, it will be necessary to write menus to fit your employee schedule. If your head cook is off on Monday, then Monday's menu should be written with few items that require a lot of advance cooking. By the same token, if your best cook in the service kitchen is off, it would be wise to reduce the number of cooked-to-order items on that menu. A good menu can help a facility in many ways, and there is much to consider in the preparation of what you will serve; there is more to it than someone's dreaming up a lot of fancy names and dishes.

Limit Menus. Just as limiting the number of items presented will help in many other departments (purchasing, receiving, storage, and handling), it will also be very helpful in reducing the preparation load and work. It has been proved many times that the main attraction is not the great number of items on the menu, but how well the food is prepared and served. If you are writing a menu for a new operation, make use of the many menu surveys that have been made to help in the selection of items that the public likes and buys. If you are in an existing operation of any type, it is a simple matter of keeping sales records and gradually eliminating those items that do not sell or are not popular. Why spend hours and waste a lot of good food in preparing a liver casserole that will not sell, or stewed eggplant, which most customers will pass by? Write the menu based on what your customers like and buy, rather than on what one individual thinks will sell and be popular. Most highly trained cooks and chefs have always cringed at the mention of a hamburger; however, it is now number one on the hit parade in America—and it isn't doing badly even in other parts of the world.

In fact, limiting the menu should go beyond those items that are difficult to prepare. An exotic fruit juice, for instance, that does not sell and just stays on the shelf should be taken from the menu. Don't waste your time and money in trying to educate your customers in what they should eat or what is good for them; let them be the judge.

Of course, this does not apply to all segments of food service—the school lunch program is interested very much in diet and in teaching children to eat the proper things; hospitals also must present a variety of diets for their patients. But in the strictly commercial area, it would be better to give the public what it wants.

Use Convenience Foods. These cover a wide area—frozen, canned, dehydrated, mixes, prefabricated, and so on—and there is a very wide selection today for everyone in the food service business. The use of such foods, of course, is a very quick easy way to reduce the preparation load and problem, and more people should realize the benefits to be gained. We still have the same old objections to overcome—"they cost too much," "they just don't taste as good as what I make," "my customers would not accept them"—most of which are just opinions. The whole processing industry that makes these products has grown by leaps and bounds and is continuing to expand, so *somebody* must like the products.

The use of these foods can help in areas other than the preparation cooking. For example, most meat items can be bought already fabricated and ready to cook and serve; being able to close down a large meat-cutting room can be very helpful to many places. The important thing is that we must consider this route in the future for the good of the food service industry. It is not a question of who is right or wrong, or changing someone's mind; it is just a simple good business tactic that must be used. The "do it yourself better and cheaper" era is beginning to weaken in our industry and in many other endeavors.

Prepare and Freeze. For those who wish to prepare their own foods, there is another way to reduce the amount of time and effort involved in making favorite recipes and dishes. It is possible now, with the new equipment available, to prepare foods in advance on premises, freeze the excess, and use it at a later time. For example, if one of the specialties of the house is Beef Burgundy, instead of making the usual two gallons needed for one day's menu, you could prepare a much larger quantity and freeze the excess, to be used the next time the dish appears on the menu. In this way, we can schedule and plan our production to fit the number of skilled help available and the hours devoted to food preparation. The food prep crew could work a normal five-day week and produce all the items needed within these limits. One restaurant I have in mind specializes in spaghetti with meat sauce. Every Monday, they make about 50 gallons of the sauce and freeze the excess to be used throughout the week; in this way, they are cooking the sauce only one day of the week rather than spending hours each day performing this task.

One word of advice. If you are planning this route, make sure that you have the proper freezing equipment. An ordinary freezer at zero degrees is not suitable for doing the freezing. One needs a special freezer set at least 40 degrees below zero for this; once the product has been quickly frozen, it can be placed in a holding box at zero or ten degrees below. Slow freezing is not advisable and explains why so many people have trouble with this process. The quicker a product is frozen and the lower the temperature (many food processors use a nitrogen process and flash freeze at 300 degrees below zero), the better it will be when it is thawed and reconstituted. Many of the unfavorable comments in our industry about frozen foods come from the fact that most do not understand how to handle them. I have eaten as many poor foods prepared from scratch in restaurants as I have eaten poor frozen or convenience foods; the words "homemade" or "baked on the premises" are no assurance that the end product will be good.

Reduce Leftovers. Years ago, all leftover foods from the day before were carefully saved, special dishes like chicken croquettes were made from them, and a flyer was placed on the menu to merchandise them the next day. Then a strange thing happened—the cost of labor and all other expenses rose to the point where this process is no longer profitable or expedient. If we added all the labor and other costs to an order of chicken croquettes today, the price would be excessive, and this is the reason items like this are not placed on menus much any more.

There are two solutions to this problem of leftovers:

1. Use more items on the menu that do not create leftover problems—items that can be used the next day without a lot of reworking and labor. If one is serving a hot turkey sandwich and using turkey breast that is sliced more or less as needed, this turkey breast can be used the next day without much preparing and cooking.

2. In using items like chicken pot pies, the answer is to plan carefully so that there will be no leftovers—in fact, many plan to run out of these items first at mealtime, to avoid the problem of handling them again the next day. Or if this item is made in advance and frozen, then it is possible to thaw and reconstitute as needed during the day, and this too will avoid a lot of leftover foods that are wasteful and expensive.

It is apparent even at this early stage that if we do a better planning and management job, many of the problems and losses that we have can be avoided in the future.

CONTROLLED PRODUCTION

Whatever route is chosen—preparing all items from scratch on premises, combining this with a few convenience items, or going mostly to convenience foods—there is need for good production control in every facility.

Establishing Amounts To Be Prepared

Management must do this job each day if waste is to be stopped. The decision on how much to prepare ahead must be based on past sales history and projections if it is to be effective. If we used three gallons of meat sauce the last time it was on the menu, and ran out two hours before dinner ended, it would surely be a good idea to increase the amount the next time. The same principle applies to the many other items sold. For instance, in the case of a Reuben sandwich, portions of corned beef, Swiss cheese, and sauerkraut are needed in advance to make this item; if we run out of the ingredients in the middle of a busy lunch, service will be slowed while someone runs back to slice and portion more of these. Without good daily and meal production control, the operation can be hurt in two ways: Too much can be produced, causing waste and loss, or too little produced, causing service troubles, delays, and running out of items, which leads to customer dissatisfaction.

Portion Control

There must be constant portion control all through the preparation of food served today. Many who claim to have this might indeed have initiated it at one time or another, but the measuring and weighing have gradually stopped, and cooks are relying on their judgment most of the time. The more expensive food becomes, the more good portion control is needed. Even in large meat-processing plants, where one man cuts strip steaks day after day, a portion scale stands on his bench at all times, and he checks the ounce weight on about every third steak to make sure the desired weight is being cut. Yet in many food service kitchens, it is hard to find a scale being used, and seldom do we provide more than one for the various stations, even though they do not cost very much.

Other portioning can be done with scoops, ladles, and other types of measuring tools. For example, in making a tuna

salad sandwich, using a #30 scoop each time constitutes portion control. If the recipe for the tuna salad calls for so much
tuna and so much celery, but the cook makes up the salad
without a recipe or even weighing or measuring the ingredients, there could be a good deal of loss.

Portion control is just as important in order to see that
the customer gets the same amount each time as it is to make
sure the facility is not giving too much food. If the ingredients
are not carefully measured each time to make that beef stew,
the product could vary from day to day, either causing loss or
making some customer unhappy because he only got two
pieces of meat. So along with portion control, we must also
have recipe control—our products must be uniform.

Cooking and Temperature Control

Another important part of food preparation that is left
to chance too often, or to a cook's judgment, is the temperature used for cooking. Most cooking appliances, such as
fryers, ranges, and ovens, come equipped with temperature
controls and thermostats, but these do not remain accurate
forever, and they must be checked and repaired quite often to
maintain accuracy.

A good example of the difference temperature can
make is in the roasting of meats. Many years ago, the theory
was that the meat should be placed first in a very hot oven for
a short time to sear it on the outside, which was supposed to
seal in the juices and reduce shrinkage; then the temperature
was to be turned down to cook it. Quite a bit of research and
testing has now proved that if we roast at low temperatures—
as low as 250°, in some cases—we can cut shrinkage by as
much as 20 percent and have a tender and moist product. We
have also learned that since no two pieces are exactly the
same size and thickness, trying to guess when a roast is done
by pressing on the exterior is not accurate, but using a meat
thermometer that shows when the proper internal temperature is reached will yield a uniform product with minimum
shrinkage and waste.

Planning for Convenience Foods

Even when frozen foods are used, there must be some advance planning for the best results. Not all products can be cooked right from the frozen state, and many require slow thawing under refrigeration (36-40°F) for periods ranging from 24 to 36 hours. However, there is one advantage here, because even after the frozen product has been thawed under refrigeration, as long as it is not cooked, it will have additional shelf life, which will cut down on losses.

Preparing Food Close to Serving Time

For many, this seems a difficult thing to do, because it does take some planning and thought. However, the longer foods must be held after cooking, the worse their quality. Much of this bad quality stems either from a shortage of cooks or from cooks who would rather prepare everything for the complete meal at one time because it is easier for them. Of the many places that feature baked potatoes, for example, quite a few bake all the potatoes needed for the entire dinner at 3 P.M. The potato served at 5 o'clock may not be so bad, but the one seved at 8 will not be in very good condition. All foods are at their peak of flavor and appeal just after being prepared; every hour they are held awaiting service will destroy some of the quality.

Although most people think only of cooking when any-one mentions food service, there are many other important considerations in successful food service, as you are beginning to see. The finest dish prepared by the most experienced chef will mean little if it doesn't reach the customer's plate in per-fect condition and if the service is not pleasant and prompt. If a great cook knows little about control and making profits, all the effort put forth will be wasted. This is why we are break-ing up the various areas within food service so that they can be analyzed and improved. All the functions must be carefully planned and then meshed perfectly to produce good results, and we must look at the whole picture.

In the matter of food preparation today, you will have quite a few choices of roads to take—and this is good, because none of us knows for sure everything that will happen in the future. One thing we must all have is an open mind—be willing to try new products, equipment, ideas, systems, and everything that will make this an even larger and better industry. As I think back over 40 years in this business and all the innovations and new ideas, I remember that the first reaction was always, "This will never work"; but strangely, many of the ideas discarded early in the game are now being widely used. The important thing is not to base decisions on opinions alone, but to get the facts and try things for yourself. Then, too, always remember the people you are serving— they have the final say on whether something is good or bad. Maybe you don't like hamburgers, but the signs in front of McDonald's prove that quite a few people are eating them.

SUMMARY

1. *Three classifications.* The food service industry can be broken down into three areas: food preparation, food service, and food serving. Once by far the most important, food preparation is now subordinated to the other two functions, because many foods are now purchased already prepared, and because the public now demands better service.

2. *Reduction of Preparation.* The amount of food preparation in a facility should be reduced as much as possible in order to improve service, reduce building space and equipment, and lower operating costs. To do this, we must balance and limit menus, make use of convenience foods, prepare large quantities and freeze the excess, and reduce leftovers.

3. *Production Control.* Amounts to be prepared and portions to be served must be controlled carefully, and recipes should be adhered to. In addition, time and temperature controls should be used in cooking, and foods should be prepared only shortly before serving time, so that they will be at the peak of their quality when served.

QUESTIONS FOR REVIEW

1. What job titles do you think the personnel have who are assigned to each of the three classifications of the food service industry, as defined in this chapter?

2. Describe and explain the shift in emphasis today from food preparation to food service.

3. Earlier in this book, several reasons were given for limiting menus. What further or more specific ones are presented in this chapter?

4. Find a convenience food—frozen or canned—in your supermarket, and make notes of the quantity, ingredients, and price. Then, using a cookbook for reference if necessary, calculate what it would cost to buy each of the ingredients in the amounts required; estimate the length of time it would take you to make it, multiplied by a given wage rate; and figure the approximate amount of gas or electricity needed to prepare it. Add up the probable costs and compare the total with the price of the convenience food. Which is more expensive?

8

Food and Beverage Service

Objectives

The ability to serve the customer quickly and well is the most important factor in success in the food service industry, as we shall see in this chapter. When he has completed it, the student should be able to:
1. Understand the importance of food service and its relationship to the other functions of the industry.
2. Describe modern methods for improving food and beverage service.
3. Plan for the proper utilization of manpower in food service.

When you are seriously ill, the first thing a doctor does is to give you a complete examination and then try to localize the trouble, so effective treatment can be started. We are doing the same thing in this introductory course—breaking down the entire operation of food service into its most important parts. This is the best way to fully understand the whole and also gives us a method for making corrections or keeping the facility on its proper course. Just as it is almost impossible for any doctor to look quickly at a patient and decide exactly what is wrong or the best course of action, when a food service operation is "sick" and needs help, it is also impossible for anyone to walk in and arrive quickly at the solution; each part must be analyzed, and then the corrections can be made in an orderly fashion.

DESCRIPTION OF FOOD SERVICE

This chapter, food and beverage service, covers the fundamentals of getting the final product to the servers—the next step following preparation. (See the definition of food service at the beginning of the preceding chapter.) Unless we can break the total down into its parts, we will not understand or be able to solve the many problems of the industry.

(Lest there be any confusion between the titles of this chapter and of Chapter 9, "Food and Beverage Serving," this chapter goes to the point where we get the end product to the server, while Chapter 9 will deal with the server's getting the product to its final goal, the consumer.)

Food and beverage service can cover all types of

service and all parts of the industry—table service, cafeteria, walk-up, buffet, tray service to hospital patients or to passengers on a plane, or lunches to schoolchildren. You will see again that there is a common denominator for all of these regarding the service of food. This is one of the most important areas of all in the industry and probably least understood by many. Your ability to serve food well and quickly will spell the difference between success and failure in any branch of the industry. All the other departments are, of course, important and must be studied, but you could have the best purchasing agent, the finest receiver, chef, accountant, or cashier, and still fail to make the grade if your service is not tops.

It is important to learn and remember that in our business, we are busy only about 20 to 25 percent of the time in operation. Naturally, these busy periods are at mealtime, whether it be breakfast, lunch, dinner, or supper. Our customers are accustomed to eating meals at certain times, and it is difficult to adjust this situation. Unlike shoe stores or supermarkets, which do business steadily through all the hours they are open, we must do the greatest part of our business in a relatively short time each day, or not at all. If you have a table-service restaurant with 100 seats and are able to serve only 150 people for lunch or 100 for dinner, or a cafeteria that can put only four or five people per minute through the line, or a school-lunch operation that can put only eight children through its line instead of 15, your sales will be low and your expenses high. Unfortunately, all our customers want to be fed at almost the same time; many of us have tried to stimulate business in midmorning or midafternoon, but the results were not very successful. If you learn and understand this one fact early in your career, you will be much better suited to successfully operate any kind of food service.

Just as the name of our industry is food *service*, not food *preparation*, your ability to produce the most dollar sales per hour or per employee, or to serve the highest number of meals, will be the key to your success. Fast service of good food not only will make your customer happy and contented, but it will also make your sales and profit look much better.

IMPROVING FOOD AND BEVERAGE SERVICE

Because this department has not always received the attention and consideration it should have, let's look at some of the things we must do to strengthen it and make it work better.

Better Planning

Most of our food service areas now in operation were either designed years ago to be operated by a large number of people, or designed by someone who did not consider this area as important as the main cooking area. Once we had a person for each job and position—a fry cook, who did nothing but the frying, a broiler man, sauté man, hot-food server, oven man— which meant that if the design and layout of the service area was not good, we could compensate by adding more cooks and other employees; "runners," for example, who spent the entire meal period running back and forth between the service area and the refrigerators and storerooms, bringing each item needed, almost one at a time. Now we must operate with much more compact kitchens, because space is at a premium, and, of course, our employees are neither as numerous nor as skilled as those that were available in the past. Because of much higher wage rates, we cannot afford to have large staffs. However, the newer kitchens, although more compact and manned by fewer people, must be able to produce as much if not more food in a given time, so there must be better planning and selection of equipment to do the job. This new and better planning is very much in evidence in all parts of the industry: fast-food operations that lead in dollar sales per employee per year and that operate with very few employees, restaurants serving thousands of dinners a night with four or five employees in the kitchen, self-service lines properly designed that can serve many more people with fewer employees. Actually, this is what productivity means—the numbers served or dollar sales in relation to the number of man-hours.

Equipment

Now we also have the equipment needed to do this job better and faster. Many years ago, the equipment used was much larger but did not have the capacity of the equipment available today. We now have deep-fat fryers, half the size of older models, that can produce more properly fried food than two of the old models did, griddles that will maintain proper temperature all through the service period without cooling, broilers that will produce the finished product in half the time, all sizes of convection ovens that also cook much faster than the conventional types, microwave ovens that cook in a very short time, compact steamers with high capacity, quartz units to heat or brown products very quickly. In short, over the years, with a lot of study and testing, the industry has come up with all the equipment needed to fit into the new compact kitchen we must have, and this equipment also does a better job and produces a much better product.

The deep-fat fryers years ago had very little heat input, and after four or five loads of food were cooked, the temperature of the cooking fat dropped to a low point and failed to recover to the proper temperature. From that point on through the meal, we were trying to fry foods at temperatures almost half of that needed, and this meant not only long frying times, but a product that was grease-soaked and unappetizing. The same thing happens when a grill fails to recover temperature; a hamburger or steak placed on a cool grill will just lie there and simmer for quite a while, resulting in another product not fit to serve.

Many in our business do not realize the importance of the proper equipment and are still trying to serve good food with old, worn-out equipment that should have been discarded years ago. Failure to keep the equipment in top condition and working order not only can hurt the quality of the food, but it can cost money as well. An old oven without correct temperature control can use an excessive amount of gas or electricity and even result in a lot of burned food. That old fryer that fails to come back to proper temperature will produce fried products that contain as much as 28 percent by weight of the fat they are cooked in. A modern fryer will reduce this absorption by as much as 20 percent; the savings in fat alone will soon pay for the new fryer, to say nothing of producing a much better product.

Another element that has been added to the newer equipment is more automation, control, and timing devices. We finally arrived at the obvious conclusion that if we could not have either the number or skill of employees we needed, the equipment must be designed and built to replace these two shortages. Now one person must do many jobs in the kitchen, not just stand in front of a fryer constantly doing one single task. A few days' practical experience in a modern service kitchen will soon prove how much the right equipment can assist in getting out good food. If one person has something in the fryer, another dish in the oven, something on the grill, and a steak in the broiler all at the same time, it is almost impossible for him to watch them all and make sure they are cooked the right length of time. For example, to properly fry frozen french fried potatoes requires about four minutes; just trying to judge this time right mentally is difficult, and of course, it is even harder when you are trying to time four or five other items at the same time. Now we have fryers with automatic lift baskets. The product is placed in a basket, then lowered into the hot fat, and lifted out automatically at the right time. Modern broilers convey the product through cooking both sides at once and, again, stop cooking at just the correct time. Much of the other equipment has automatic timers that signal when the right moment has arrived.

Many in the industry think these things are just "gadgets" and not worth the additional money, but this belief stems mainly from the fact that they do not understand the complexity and difficulty of what must be done today.

A third important development in the newer equipment is that much of it is now either self-cleaning or much easier to clean. Again, many in the industry do not consider this to be of much importance, but anyone who has spent hours trying to clean an oven or hand-scrape a grill or broiler can appreciate this feature. At today's wage rates, several hours a day saved on cleaning the equipment can amount to a considerable sum at the end of the year. In addition, dirty, crusted equipment wastes a lot of heat and energy, and cleaning is a job that no one enjoys, so if we can eliminate only a part of this task, we have made a step forward.

Ample Supplies Where Needed

If we still had our "runners," described earlier, location of supplies would not be such an important consideration; but we have lost the "runners," so we must consider and understand what is meant by supplies, or "backup."

The main job of the preparation department is to see

that the food service area is properly supplied with all the foods needed for a given serving period or length of time. If the one, two, or three employees working in this area at the busiest time of the day must stop every minute or so to run back to the walk-in boxes or storeroom, or take five minutes to slice some more ham or make some more potato salad, then the speed of service is slowed quite a bit. When we must serve hundreds of people in a very short space of time, it is essential to start thinking in terms of minutes, or even seconds, considering all the dishes that must be prepared and set up for service. That five-minute delay because someone had to slice some more ham could mean that you served ten fewer people that day for lunch; constantly running out of backup food for self-service lines could reduce the number served per minute from eight to seven, and again affect the total number served. How many times have you gone through a cafeteria line when an item has run out and the whole line must wait until someone runs to the back of the kitchen to replenish? The key to faster service is saving all those unnecessary steps and cutting away those wasted seconds and minutes.

Those sales records we have mentioned before are the key to knowing how much of everything to prepare and stock the service kitchen with. Then we must consider having these supplies where needed. If the refrigerator for the meat to be grilled or broiled is at one end of the area and the equipment at the other, one can imagine all the needless walking just for one meal period. Move the refrigerator closer to the grill and eliminate those steps; on the self-service line, have the backup hot- and cold-food units directly behind the line, so that replenishing will be faster and done with far fewer steps. It is amazing how just a few needless steps can add up in a period of time.

Some years ago, a study was made of in-flite meal service on airplanes. It was found that on a plane with about 100 passengers, with a system of serving only two trays per trip from the galley, the average stewardess walked about five miles to serve one luncheon. As explained earlier, we as an industry may not rank very high in productivity, but we certainly are way up there in the excessive walking department, and the important consideration here is that our employees are not producing when they are walking.

More Supervision

In the chapter on food preparation, it was brought out that that department has always comprised the most-skilled and highest-paid employees. This was reasonable, since that type of work does require more training and experience. But usually, when the chef or cook had finished making the entrees for the day, the butcher had cut all the meat, and the baker finally taken all the baked products from the oven, they were through—their jobs were completed. From then on, it was up to others to take these foods and serve them. Because most of the payroll money had been spent in preparation, there was not much left for the employees on the service line, so less-skilled and lower-paid employees had to be utilized. Most of the people in management also assumed that when they had done all their work and seen that the service kitchen was set up, they could relax and do some office work or something else in the back of the house. As a result, we ended up with a lot of hard-working, well-meaning employees trying to get food into the hands of servers quickly under very trying conditions.

Because we have only that short time in which to get those dollars or serve all those meals, it would be wise to throw all the employees and talent into the service kitchen for that two-hour lunch or dinner period. If those in the service kitchen cannot serve fast enough or handle the food properly, then all the work done in the rear will amount to little. A chef can make a delicious soup, but if someone doesn't see that it is heated properly just before serving by turning on the soup warmer at the right time, the soup will be cold when served, and the customer will not be happy. The butcher may cut a top-quality sirloin strip steak, but if the person running the broiler cooks it well done when it has been ordered rare, again we have failed to score with the customer.

One of the large supermarkets has a slogan about the

sale not being complete until the food is eaten; this could be a good slogan for the food service industry as well. They say that what makes a champion is that he can go that extra distance or put forth some additional effort. We too must make sure that we go all the way and have that follow-through right to the customer—that extra effort can be the difference between success and failure. Waiting lines during meal periods in most types of food service do not necessarily mean that more seats are needed; they may be a good indication that the food service needs speeding up a bit. If the service is slow and you add more seats, all you are doing is making the guest wait at the table instead of in line.

Not only must we put our first team of skilled personnel into action during the rush period; they should start in advance by carefully checking everything to make sure that they are ready for the busy period. In fact, if this is not done thoroughly each day, even those highly skilled employees will have trouble serving the food. One very large, successful chain realized so well the importance of everyone's concentrating on the service period that they would allow no phone calls to the unit from the main office during serving times— they wanted to make sure that the attention of all the employees was on that most vital time of the day.

Faster and Better Control

One of the major tasks connected with the service of food is control and accounting—writing the checks, placing the orders, tallying the trays if the place is self-service, collecting the cash, and all the other work entailed in this function. If old-fashioned hand methods are used and a good system not devised, there are bound to be delays and trouble with the service. It is essential that all branches of food service get paid for what they produce, whether the payment is based on money received or meals served, and unless better ways are initiated to record these transactions, the entire system will be in trouble.

If the servers have difficulty writing, pricing, extending, and totaling the checks, a great deal of time is lost; if the cashier at the end of a self-service line is slow in tallying items sold or collecting money as the trays come through, the entire turnover is slowed; if a cook in the service kitchen cannot read the check turned in, then everything must be held until the difficulty can be solved. These may seem like small matters, but they do have a big effect on the speed and efficiency of service. In one instance I watched, a school-lunch service was set up to produce 30 trays a minute, but each child had to pay cash for his or her lunch, and the cashier could handle only six transactions a minute, so the whole process slowed to six trays a minute.

More Skilled Help

As we have seen, for years, most of the highly skilled and trained help has been used in the back of the house in food preparation. This practice did not leave much for the front food service, which was thought to require far less skill and knowledge. Now we are beginning to realize that better employees are needed to serve the food if we are to improve the quality of the food and speed the service.

The designation most often given for the employees in the food service area is "short-order cook," but there is much more involved now than in the past. More and more menus are featuring this cooked-to-order food, and naturally, this work has increased, calling for more skilled and able servers. Years ago, most of the food served came off the steam table. We served more already-prepared items because it was faster, and actually we did not have very good "short-order" equipment. Most of the entrees were roasts, stews, casseroles, loaves—items that were already cooked and needed only to be dished up in a hurry, very similar to the items being served on cafeteria lines today. This type of food, of course, required much more preparation and precooking than the items we find now. Now the emphasis seems to be on fried, broiled, grilled, and sautéed foods; the public prefers these, according to the menu tallies and menu popularity polls.

In brief, the cooking and serving load has switched from preparation and advance cooking up to the front line, or

service kitchen. Very few people in this "short-order" work have ever received much formal training; this was always considered an easy job that did not require much talent, since the chef had already done all the hard work. However, this is not the case. Many of the staff now in service kitchens came up through the ranks—usually from the dishwashing or pot washing section—when someone failed to report for work one day or resigned, and the dishwasher was suddenly shifted to the service kitchen. There is nothing wrong with the system of promoting from within, but to be suddenly thrown into a job like this without any experience or training is hard on a person. Once he started the job, it was mostly left up to him to learn everything possible by himself, or to seek the advice of someone else—who usually did not know much about what should be done.

We must realize that these are the cooks that are doing the final cooking and making up the various dishes that the customer sees and eats; in other words, they have the greatest responsibility for the final end product. If they are not properly trained in all sections of the service kitchen, how can we expect the food served to be right? The same is true of the dining areas; you can have the greatest manager or hostess in the world, but it is the server who has the most direct contact with the customer. If the server is poorly trained, inefficient, surly, or unfit for the job, then once again, all has been lost.

We must learn to zero in on what is important in our industry—who actually does have the greatest direct effect on and contact with the guest. I have been eating in all types of food service operations for over 40 years and can count on one hand the times when I came in contact with the manager or chef to any degree, but I can cite many times when I had bad service or poor food because someone in the service kitchen did not know what he was doing. A great deal of skill and knowledge is needed for this type of work, if it is done right. The next time you are in a restaurant kitchen and have the opportunity, ask some questions like these:

"What is the best temperature for frying?"

"How long does it take to correctly fry an order of frozen french fried potatoes, or a frozen veal cutlet?"

"What is the best griddle temperature for eggs? for hot cakes? for meats?"

"How many times do you turn a hamburger over during the cooking?"

"During the rush period, is it a good idea to turn up the temperatures on broilers, grills, and fryers?"

"Do you season meats before broiling or grilling, or salt fried products when taken from the hot grease?"

You will get either a great variety of answers or none at all, because most personnel have never been taught how to do this job right. If this type of cooking is so simple, why have so many fast-food ventures failed over the years? We say that anyone can cook a hamburger, hot cakes, or eggs, but actually very few know how to do these things right. There is a right way—a correct temperature, a right length of time—for each of these foods, and it is time our management became aware of the need for more training, instruction, and supervision of what has always been considered a job that anyone can do without training or supervision.

Expeditors

Expeditiors will be mentioned and discussed in other parts of the course, but when we are talking about the food service kitchen, this subject is of major importance. The dictionary defines *expedite* as "to hasten the process or progress of"; this is exactly what we need in the food service kitchen and servers' aisle.

At every meal or rush period, someone from management or in a key position should station himself in the area where the food is being served and picked up, to supervise and control the entire operation. If guest checks are used, this person can take the checks from the servers and call in the orders, to avoid any bickering and confusion between the cooks and servers. The expeditor can also control the advance cooking of food, coordinate the orders being filled so that the server gets the complete order on time, see that all departments and jobs are covered throughout the meal period, and see that the serving ware is being supplied as needed.

In addition to speeding service and increasing sales, this person would also be in a position to see that the food is being served correctly—in short, to make sure the customer is getting quality food on time. Management must be where the action is and when it is happening if the operation is to run smoothly and be successful. Once the service system runs amok and things get out of control, it is very difficult to come in and straighten out the mess; the best solution is to be there and see that no mess happens.

Bars and Lounges

Much has also been happening in recent years to improve the service of beverages or alcoholic drinks. Once, the bartender was solely responsible for working out his own systems and procedures, but gradually management began to realize that improvements could be made, so research was undertaken. The modern bar, with new equipment and service methods, is certainly a far cry from the old-time saloon-type bar.

This is a very profitable part of the food service industry, and certainly deserves all the attention possible. In the process of developing systems to ensure proper control of drinks and better dispensing equipment, it was learned that the productivity of bartenders could be greatly increased and service speeded. Now we have portion-control systems that accurately dispense the right amount of liquor in an instant and also record the sales. In fact, one system has gone to the point that when the check is rung, the drinks are automatically mixed. We also have very fine hand or bar-top dispensing heads that instantly dispense mixers such as soda, ginger ale, quinine water, and so on; better draft-beer systems; and we can even pump bulk wines at the right temperature to be drawn and served quickly. We have eliminated all those bottles that had to be handled, chilled, and then disposed of. We have fine new glass-washing machines that can be installed in bars to quickly wash glasses clean, instead of the bartender's just swishing them in a sinkful of dirty water, and ice machines that deliver ice on the spot, rather than having someone carry it in by the bucket. In fact, a modern bar today, with the right equipment and setup, can enable one person to serve from two to three times as many people and do a better job.

Again, it has been argued that the customer does not like all these newfangled things, but this is just the opinion of a few and is not based on fact. The truth of the matter is that the customer couldn't care less *how* you do the job; he is interested in getting a good product, served right, and quickly. A good drink must be made to formula just like a fine food dish; trying to do it by guesswork, and assuming that one can determine down to the quarter of an ounce by sight only, does not produce the best product.

This part of our industry has needed improving for many years, and it is fortunate that there were a few brave souls who did something about it. If you can reduce beverage costs by 2 to 5 percent and double the speed of service, it pays to look into the matter.

Menus Fit to the Facility

One of the biggest problems in all types of food service operations is that the menu does not fit either the physical plant, the equipment, or the skill of the employees. Management may think that the more items offered, the greater the sales and profits, but actually, the reverse happens. This does not mean that you cannot add items to your menu, but you must have the space, equipment, and know-how to serve them properly. If you want to feature a special fish-fry night, fine; but make sure you have the number of fryers needed, a place to dump the product and season it, and employees who know how to handle the fried fish correctly. Adding a Reuben sandwich to the menu could be a good idea, but make sure you have a place for all the ingredients needed, and the right kind of double grill to handle it.

Unless you strengthen the facility and the employees' ability, it would be better to stay with what you have—or, if you add something, to drop a slow-moving item to better balance the load. Every kitchen has a certain peak capacity; when you demand more of it, there will be trouble and, in most instances, a drop in sales and profits.

SUMMARY

1. *Definition.* Food service is the function that takes the food from the preparation stage to the server, and also involves "short-order" cooking. Efficiency in this function is essential to success.

2. *Shift in Emphasis.* Because of the current shortage of manpower, and also because the modern consumer tends to prefer broiled and grilled foods, it is necessary today to place much greater reliance on food service than we did in the past. We must increase both the skill of the personnel in this area and the efficiency of the function itself.

3. *Improvements.* Many methods are available for improving food service: better planning, more efficient equipment, and excellent control systems. In addition, management must provide constant supervision, including the use of expeditors during busy periods.

QUESTIONS FOR REVIEW

1. What changes in the public's taste have contributed to the current emphasis on food service as opposed to food preparation?

2. List the advantages of replacing an old-style deep-fat fryer with a new one that has automatic controls for temperature and timing.

3. In what ways can a good control system aid in speed and efficiency of food service?

4. What is the role of an "expeditor" in food service?

9

Food and Beverage Serving

Objectives

Most customer complaints in the food service industry have to do with deficiencies in the area of serving. After reading this chapter, the student should know:

1. The definition of serving, with its two components.
2. Ways to facilitate serving, to benefit both the servers and the customers.
3. Methods of combining types of service in the same facility.

As we have seen, when we departmentalize all the various functions in the total job and break them down into smaller segments, it is much easier to check the parts and locate the problems. The way to solve any problem is to first diagnose or define, then take steps to correct.

When one has bad service, it is important to discover the what and where of the cause—we cannot blame the servers or the people working on serving lines if they can't get the food from the kitchen on time. By the same reasoning, if the kitchen's are performing well and we still have bad service, then we know to look into the actual serving areas themselves. We must be able to find the source of the trouble in any part of the business before we can make adjustments and corrections.

DEFINITION

Good serving involves two things:

1. Getting the food or beverage to the customer promptly or when he is ready for it

2. Completeness—that is, making sure the guest has everything needed

Nothing is as irritating to a customer as waiting in long, slow-moving self-service lines or sitting at a table waiting for his or her food. Only a few minutes' delay can seem like an eternity to someone waiting to be served. In fact, if there is a direct complaint, the guest will usually say that he waited 20 or 30 minutes when the actual delay was only 5. The important thing is not the actual difference in time, but the fact that even very short delays can cause the guest to be annoyed and upset.

The other very serious problem in this area is the lack of complete service, and this causes the most trouble. It involves the server forgetting to provide all the small items needed to enjoy the meal—perhaps the guest finds no napkins, or no salt on the table, or the server brings the steak but forgets the steak knife or the sauce requested, serves the soup but forgets to include the crackers or the soup spoon, brings coffee but no cream, pie but no fork. In some table-service restaurants, it is difficult to even to get a menu when you are seated. These small things can be even more annoying than slow service of the main items. And it is very difficult in most places to get someone's attention to bring the missing items. Much of this problem can be traced to poor training of the servers, but a lot of it is also due to the fact that these items are not readily available to the servers when and where needed.

We all recognize that the food must be good, but many fail to realize that if the guest is upset by a lot of little serving annoyances, he is not going to enjoy the meal, no matter how excellent its quality. There are many things that management can do to overcome these problems; we will touch on a few of them in this chapter, and more in later chapters.

SERVING CONSIDERATIONS

Let's look at a few of the main considerations in this matter of proper serving.

Control

Control is placed at the head of the list because it is of such great importance to the business. We must be sure to get paid for all the items served, or proper tally figures where money is not involved. This control must come at the time the food is served, not at a later time, as most think. Once the loss has happened, it is too late to go back and recoup. In addition, why waste all that valuable time poring over records and checks to find an error that cannot be corrected, when you could have prevented the mistake from happening?

If the guest checks are not written properly, cannot be read, are extended wrong, are added incorrectly, or have items omitted, or if the cashier at the end of the self-service line misses many items, then there will be significant losses that cannot and will not be recovered later. The same thing applies to beverage service—if a good control system is lacking here, again there can be serious loss to management and owners. Failure to charge can be intentional on the server's part, for the sake of receiving higher tips, but there can also be a lot of unintentional errors that hurt the profit just as much.

Fortunately, we do have excellent control systems now; the point is that our people must use them. In fact, some of these modern control systems not only ensure that you are getting your money, but actually help to speed service. They necessitate less time spent taking the order, provide checks that are easier to read and to fill from the service kitchen, automatically extend prices, total them, including the tax, make them easier for the cashier to handle, and, even more important, give itemized counts of all items sold. In brief, they are of great assistance in all areas of food service.

Getting the Proper Order

In most cases, this is where the servers' troubles start—in not picking up the correct item to be served. This is why it is so important to have someone in authority supervise the service, especially during the busy periods, in order to eliminate these mistakes before they happen and save a lot of running back and forth to deliver the right item. Not only do we have the problem of getting the right item to the right server, but the server must be able to pick up everything needed to serve a party. In most instances, a party of guests at a table will order a variety of items, and when the time comes to serve, if the steak and fish are ready but the salad is not, there is a delay until the salad is fixed. If the two items that are ready are served and the third person is told that his order is not ready, this again is poor service. If there is no one to supervise pickup, another server may pick up that salad, and this will break up the sequence. Or perhaps a full order is ready, but the kitchen has run out of baked potatoes. This means that the server must make an additional trip to the table to find out what the guest would like instead, and meanwhile, everyone at the table must wait until the additional item is delivered.

These are all small matters individually, but they annoy customers and can drive away business. They are easily corrected, and they must be.

Well-Stocked Supply Areas

Supply areas, usually called service stands, in most instances are too small and do not carry enough supplies for good service. Once again, most of the attention of designers and planners has been the kitchen—first it was to establish a large and expensive preparation kitchen, then attention shifted to the service kitchen—but not much effort has been put into proper service areas and equipment. Many of the plans end up with two or three small stands, crowded into a corner where they cannot be seen, which are expected to take care of the needs of the servers.

First of all, in the average place, there are approximately 50 items of service, over and above the drink or food that comes from the service areas, that must be convenient and ready for the servers: glasses, flatware, china, napkins, place mats, linens, condiments, beverages, dressings, butter, rolls, and so on. So it is easy to see that considerable space is needed to stock an adequate supply of all these materials to ensure proper service.

Actually, in many instances, the service kitchen should be smaller than the serving pickup area, because in most of the service kitchens, we are using as few as two people, and they do not need much room to operate. Then, too, with the newer limited menus, the service kitchen does not have to stock the variety of items needed by the servers. If we have only two or three people in the service kitchen, how can we expect 12 or 14 servers to operate from a much smaller area? If 12 servers are lined up trying to get water and ice from one small space, the general service will be slower. If there is room for only about 24 glasses at the station, the supplying of this necessary item will become quite a problem. These serving areas must be larger, and must include space for tray setdown and ample stocks of everything where needed.

Some managers have told me that they do not worry about this problem, but leave it up to the servers. However, this is definitely a problem for management, since most of the benefits for improvement will accrue to the operation, not just to the servers. One very simple way management can help where service problems abound is to sit down with the servers and ask them what needs to be done. They will soon tell you where the weak spots are, and often, by means of only minor corrections made at very little cost, the situation can improve for everyone.

Continuity in Self-Service

Just as an army can move only as fast and far as its supply lines, self-service operations are only as good as *their* supply lines. Frequent runouts of items on the service line or long delays in restocking can slow down service to a point where they will hurt the sales and thereby the profits.

In most cafeterias, the items available are listed on a board where people in line can determine ahead of time what they want. But nothing is so aggravating as to arrive at the point of service only to find that that item has run out, or that there will be a long wait while more is prepared, This affects not only the customer involved, but also the people behind him. In a fast-food operation, it someone fails to thaw enough hamburger patties in advance, and frozen patties must be cooked in the middle of a busy period, quite a bit will be lost in sales because of the added cooking time for each burger. Good prompt service in all parts of our business depends mainly on attention to a great many small details; each of them might seem not very important, but add up all those wasted seconds and minutes, and the total results can be very harmful.

Ours is a business that needs precision and attention to detail. After all, we have only a brief time in which to do business—to serve and take in the money—and if we are slowed for any reason at all, there will be a loss that can never be made up. If the man buying a car doesn't buy it today, he may be back later, so the sale is not necessarily lost. This is not true in the food service business. That one sale you failed to make can never be recouped.

Removal of Soiled Ware and Resetting

Because most of us keep our attention on only the cooking or the service, we fail to realize that clearing the tables—getting the soiled materials back to the warehandling, and quickly resetting the table—can be most important to increasing the speed of service and the turnover. Many times, we do not even supply the proper equipment to help with this job—no carts, trays that are too small, no supply of clean wipe cloths, clean service ware placed where it is hard to get to— and thus we have placed obstacles in the path of cleanup rather than helping the problem. Not only are tables full of soiled dishes an eyesore to the new arrivals, but the longer that table sits there full of dirty dishes, the more money you are losing.

Study this part of your operation carefully to see just how you can speed the process. For example, in the area of self-service, it has always been a problem for the guest to arrive at the table, balance the tray on the edge, and remove each item and place it on the table. Then comes the problem of what to do with the empty tray; usually, it is put on a nearby table, causing a problem for the next party. Some years ago, a trapezoid tray was invented. Four of these will fit nicely on the average table, leaving room for the condiments, and so forth, so the guest can just place the entire tray on the table and eat from it without removing all the items. When it comes time to clear the table, the four trays with the dishes on them

can be quickly picked up and removed, saving the time of removing each item from the table separately—and besides, the
table probably needs less wiping with this system.

I once visited a very fine restaurant that had had special, very attractive and decorative tables built. The orders were delivered on a tray that slid into position in front of the guest; at clean-up time, these trays were removed, and the table was quickly prepared for the next guest.

Many of us say that there is nothing we can do about a lot of our problems. Not true—there is much we can do in the future to help the industry in many ways, but it does take a little thought and effort!

Wasted Steps

Some years ago, I worked for a very large chain that had service problems, as do most places. We decided to investigate and find out what was causing the delay. Each day at lunch, we observed and timed closely, and we started to count the number of trips the servers made to a table to serve one party a lunch. To our surprise, the average number of trips was thirteen! Trying to find a menu—coming back to take the order—returning to take dessert orders—forgetting to leave the check—making two trips for the coffee instead of one—forgetting the cream, the spoon—getting catsup and mustard—and on and on. Shortly before that, I had visited several restaurants in California and noticed that the servers used carts instead of trays, brought the entire order at one time, including the beverages. At the most, these servers were making three trips to the table, as against thirteen. It is easy to see that this would make quite a difference. This cart service requires more aisle space and additional dining room area, but if you can serve guests faster with fewer trips, your turnover will be greater, the service better, and sales higher. Packing a lot of tables and chairs into a small area without room to serve or have the needed items does not mean your sales will be greater; in many instances this overcrowding can slow service and, of course, make the server's job more difficult. Another helpful item is the plate cover; most think that the reason for their use is to keep the food hot, but actually their main advantage is in making it possible to safely stack four or even more plates or platters on a tray without messing up the food, so a full order can be carried in one trip instead of two or more.

Counter service is supposed to be faster than table service, but in many cases it is slower. One of the main reasons is that most counter servers carry everything by hand—two plates at a time, or only two cups of coffee at a time. But in another restaurant I visited, the counter servers used small trays and were able to bring out much more at one time, thus reducing their trips and increasing the speed of service.

There is so much we can do to improve our service that one hardly knows where to start. The best beginning would be to discard many of the old-fashioned ideas about food serving and try some new ones. One owner told me that he liked the idea of service carts, but his dining room was not large enough. He was using an 18″ x 24″ oval tray; if he didn't have room enough for an 18″ x 24″ service cart that would carry two to three times as much food, how could he have room to set down that tray and serve the tables? For many inexperienced servers, the only answer was to set the tray down on the table and hand out the items—not a very nice way to serve. Another owner agreed with the idea of plate covers but said the servers would not be able to tell what was under them. Since he had never investigated the idea, he didn't know these covers are now made in a see-through plastic, as well as in metal.

From actual surveys and time and motion studies made over the years, it would be safe to say that managers of the average food service operation could reduce the walking and number of trips by at least 50 percent if they chose to. And if they did, not only would they increase their turnover and sales, but the servers would be able to spend more time in the dining area where they belong, taking care of the guests' needs. "I'm sorry, that's not my table" has become a very funny gag line in the entertainment world, but it is not funny when you are trying to get another cup of coffee or a spoon.

Utilizing Servers

Too many of us are bound by old systems and methods and opinions—we can't make changes because of this or that;

the customer would not like it. But how do we know if we haven't tried?

One of the common ideas is that the customer wants one server to serve all the food and handle the whole transaction. I personally don't care who brings me what when I eat, as long as somebody does. Even now in very posh restaurants, one might get service from the maître d', the captain, the waiter, the wine steward, and the bus boys. If this service is accepted, why can't we have two or three different people waiting on a table at an ordinary place? Anyone could take the order, and when it was ready, someone else could deliver it.

This system, when it was finally developed by car service in fast food, reduced the number of servers considerably and increased sales. A system like this could be devised for table service, so that instead of all the servers running back and forth, some could be left in the dining areas and others could place the orders and bring out the food when it was ready.

On a plane now, a beverage cart is pushed down the aisle, and orders are taken, drinks served, and cash collected with just one trip. Contrast this with the old system, in which the stewardess took an order from one seat, ran to the back, filled the order, returned, took the next order, and ran back again—think of all those needless trips for lack of a little more system. Maybe it is time for us to examine what we are doing and come up with more new ideas.

Beverage Serving

Beverage serving has been made easier not only on planes, but in many of the more modern designs for bars and lounges. Years ago, a service bar meant taking out one or two stools at the end of the bar, and installing in their place two curved rails so that one server had room to approach the bar and get drinks to be served. Now, depending on volume of business, many places have separate service bars in addition to the sit-down one, or they have allowed much more space for the service bar attached to the regular bar.

To speed service, stands equipped with ice, glasses, trays, napkins, drink garnishes, and a dispenser for carbonated beverages are established. The server places the order, then sets up the glasses, ice, garnishes, and carbonated drinks so that, in many cases, all the bartender has to do is hand out the portion of liquor. Also, as explained under warehandling, some bars are installing automatic glasswashers, so the server can place the glass on the belt and it is quickly washed and ready for use again.

This sharing of the work load by many instead of putting it all on one produces much faster service with fewer employees, which is the goal in increasing productivity. Then, too, the bars themselves are now much easier and more convenient to work, eliminating many of the needless steps and motions of years ago.

Various Types of Service

There are many kinds and types of service in the industry, and all should be studied for possibilities:

Conventional table service

Preparation at the table (display cookery)

Buffet

Smorgasbord

Fast-food window service—walk-up

Snack Bars

Take-out or take-home

Service to the car

Drive-up window

Cafeteria

Vending

Catering

Complete tray to patients

The list could go on, but these are enough to show the many varieties of serving methods in the industry. Each type has its own advantages and purposes, and it is up to management to decide what would be best for its own establishment and clientele. Self-service, whether buffet or cafeteria, is the fastest and will handle the most customers in a given time. From there we can go all the way to preparation at the table, which, of course, would take the most time and serve the smallest number of people per hour. The type chosen depends mainly on the number to be served, but often, a place does so much business that the physical setup seems to call for a change in service during some periods, or for the entire time.

It is possible to combine many of these various systems to advantage. Many now are using the buffet combined with table service, to feed more customers in a short time. Some cafeterias have the "open shopping" arrangement. Instead of having everyone queue up in one line, the food is arranged in sections or areas in an open square, and the customer can go to the section desired for exactly what he or she wants. Some have put in a small fast-food unit for those who might want just a sandwich and salad. Many in-plant setups use vending to fill in for those slack times of the day when it is not practical to open the main cafeteria. Quite a few table-service restaurants today are using salad bars, where the customer gets his own salad and dressing to his liking. Many cafeterias station employees at the end of the line to carry the trays to the tables for the customers. An innovation in the drive-up operation is interesting in that the customer calls in his order upon approaching the place, and by the time he reaches the building and window, the food is ready.

Not only do we have a great variety of different serving methods, but we can make even more combinations of these to exactly fit the operation and the job to be done. One small downtown restaurant had a huge luncheon business and a smaller night business; to adjust to this, they served the food cafeteria style at lunchtime and used table service at night, with all the trimmings. The important thing to learn is that we are not bound to serve one certain way just because it has always been done this way—we are free to choose our own methods and even to invent new ones if we want. We must recognize the fact that there are many complaints about service in our industry, and we should strive to do a much better job in the future, no matter the system.

Anything done to improve service benefits everyone concerned—the owners and management, the servers, and, most important of all, the paying guest. Faster service will not only make all these people happier; it will make those profits and budget figures look a lot better. Much of the industry's advancement in the future will depend on directing effort and attention to the right places—putting the emphasis where it belongs.

SUMMARY

1. *Components of Food Serving.* Good serving includes both promptness and completeness. Even the best meal will not satisfy the customer if he is kept waiting for it, or if the server neglects to bring the full order or any of the serving ware he needs.

2. *Causes of Poor Serving.* Common faults in serving stem from lack of controls, errors in pickup, inadequate supply areas, bottlenecks in self-service, delays in table resetting, wasted steps by servers, and the custom of using only one server for each table.

3. *Facilitation.* A good control system can eliminate many of these faults. Also, there should be supervision of pickup; enlargement of supply areas; continuity in self-service; the use of new devices that speed cleanup and reseting, and permit the serving of many items simultaneously; the utilization of several servers per table; and up-to-date methods of beverage serving.

4. *Combinations of Service.* Not only should a facility determine the best type of service for its operation; it may well be to its advantage to combine two or more types, for the purpose of serving more customers in less time.

QUESTIONS FOR REVIEW

1. What are the two main customer complaints about food serving?

2. A common bottleneck in serving is the service stand. How can this situation be improved?

3. Name several ways that serving can be speeded up in a table-service facility; in a self-service place; at a buffet.

4. Several methods of combining types of service are given in this chapter. Can you think of others that might be advantageous to a given operation?

10

Warehandling

Objectives

Although it has in the past received little attention, warehandling is a very important function in the food service industry. The student who has read this chapter should be able to:
1. Enumerate the tasks involved in warehandling.
2. Describe the effects of having this function done poorly.
3. Name several items of equipment and several measures that can be taken to improve the efficiency of warehandling.

It may seem strange that a whole chapter of this text is devoted to warehandling, because, like the subject of how to properly boil or scramble an egg, this function has until recently been passed over lightly, for a number of reasons:

1. Most in the industry do not realize the importance of warehandling.

2. They do not realize the great amount of work and effort involved.

3. They do not realize that improper warehandling can be very costly and have serious effects on the entire operation.

4. They have never given it much thought.

5. They do not understand what is involved, or the best way to accomplish the job.

6. In most planning, this is the last department considered; it is usually given the space that is left after everything else has been figured.

In other words, as they would treat the matter of how best to handle trash and garbage, most people in authority would just as soon skip dish and pot washing and hope that someone else will solve the problem. Usually, the solution is left up to the "dishwasher" or "pot washer," who is hired on the spur of the moment and thrown into the job immediately, with very little training or help. It becomes a case of the blind leading the blind—the new man is shown to the area and told to go to work, and if he has any questions, the answers come from another employee who is himself not sure how the job should be done.

Actually, the terms "dishwashing," "dishwasher," and "pot washer" should be eliminated from the industry; not only are they confusing, but the terms themselves have caused difficulties in hiring and keeping employees in this job. Very few people today would want to tell their friends that they are "dishwashers" or "pot washers." Here again we are out of balance. We hire someone to operate what is probably the most expensive equipment in the entire operation, someone who must handle thousands and thousands of dollars' worth of very expensive serving ware, who is responsible for sanitation, who keeps the entire service going—and we pay the lowest wage in the industry, provide the least training, and give the position a very bad title. All this is unnecessary today, because modern warehandling, like bartending, has come of age. We need far fewer people to do the job, so there is no reason that the title and the wage cannot be changed.

I talked with one operator recently who was proud of the fact that he had had the same dishwasher for twelve years; her hourly rate was way below the minimum, and he had never given her a raise in all that time. This is an extreme case, but it is time we took a good look at this part of our business and did some changing and improving.

DESCRIPTIONS OF THE JOB

First, let's see what is involved in warehandling. One thing for sure, you will learn that it is far more than just dishwashing.

1. The job involves pots, pans, utensils, china, glassware, flatware, trays, and other serving equipment. The total cost of all these items for any food service operation, plus the cost of the washing equipment, amounts to a sizable amount of money.

2. All this soiled ware must be transported from its

point of use to the washing machines or sinks; this involves, for example, clearing the tables and getting the items back to the washing area, and getting the pans and utensils there from the cooks' stations.

3. All these items must be prepared for washing and sanitizing, by properly sorting, soaking, and racking.

4. They must be washed and removed from sinks or machines.

5. They must be sorted, stacked, and returned to the points of use as quickly as possible.

All these activities must be planned and coordinated into one task or function. It is a single total operation that must be well planned if it is to work.

Certainly, the job as listed above does not sound like the job description for a "dishwasher," and it isn't. In fact, this total job is the single biggest task or function in food service, not only from the point of view of cost, but in total effort and time involved. Once we realize its importance, we can take steps to solve the problems and eliminate much of the work. Not doing this job right can be very costly:

1. It can cause many wasted and unnecessary man-hours.

2. It can create very high replacement costs, owing to breakage, etc.

3. Bad warehandling can slow the service of the entire operation, reduce sales, and cause poor service.

4. It can result in the use of chipped, cracked, or dirty service ware that will also drive away customers.

5. It is the cause for much of the contamination and bacteria problems in the industry.

In fact, the productivity and ability to serve the entire facility depends to a great extent on the ability of this department to produce. Cooks cannot work effectively unless they have the pans and utensils needed; the serving line or the servers are unable to produce unless they have something to serve in—if there are no clean spoons, it is impossible to serve even a cup of coffee.

The two biggest complaints from servers are (1) not being able to get their food soon enough from the kitchen, and (2) not having the service equipment available and in the right place when they need it. We must realize that these employees depend mostly on tips for their income, and if they cannot serve a certain number of customers or parties in a very short time, their income is affected. Just from observation, we can tell when the servers are having difficulties in this respect, by watching them run from place to place to find a piece of equipment they need and end up by going back to the washing area to get it.

MAIN FEATURES OF THE AREA

Warewashing areas can be unsightly and noisy if they are not efficient and workable. However, properly designed and worked, they can be very orderly and quiet in operation. Without going into great detail yet about the mechanics and proper design for these facilities, let us examine some of the main considerations.

Location

The proper location of this department is extremely important in relationship to the rest of the operation. As we have already pointed out, there is a great amount of work, effort, and steps involved in warehandling, so anything we can do to reduce this work load will be worthwhile.

Because many improperly designed warehandling areas in the past were so noisy and unsightly, they were placed as far as possible from the very functions they were supposed to support. This meant that all the ware had to be carried to and from this area over a long distance, which in itself created much extra and wasted effort. But one very successful chain put its warewashing operation right out front, where the public could see it! This was a good idea, because it was located where it was most needed and, since it was operated very well, the public did not mind watching how their utensils were cleaned and sanitized.

Many operations today run this department only between meals; they have enough clean serving ware on hand and in place to run through the entire meal. This practice has three advantages: Because they have enough ware, the service is fast and not interrupted; they can use the employees who normally run the machines to help with the service during the rush hours, which is the imporant work; and the machines, which use a lot of hot water, soap, and power, are run for only limited times during the day rather than continuously.

Warehandling areas should be centralized, to be as close as possible to the departments they support, not way back in some corner. In some recent studies involving the school-lunch program, it was discovered that if the flite-type machine used for washing the trays was properly located, the students could place their own trays in it; the machine washed the trays, conveyed them back to the start of the serving line, and automatically stacked them ready for use again right at the point where they were needed. All this can be done with no one operating the machine, which is a very important consideration when help is so short. Bars now can be arranged so that the servers in the lounge can place the soiled glasses on a machine that will wash them and deliver them to the bartender, ready to use again where he needs them. If planned correctly, warewashing units can be placed almost anywhere, so they should be centrally located to reduce the handling problem.

Size and Design of Machines

A great deal of study and research has been and is being done on the job of warehandling. As has been explained, this is the single largest task in any food service operation, involving as it does many hours of work, the most important aid to faster service, and, of course, potentially a great added operating expense for breakage and replacement.

There are many companies in the business of manufacturing dishwashing machines, and a very large number of models in all sizes to choose from. The machines are rated in terms of so many racks or pieces per hour, and it was formerly believed that the criterion for selection was the size of the machine—determine your needs and choose the size that matches them. If you were having trouble with your warehandling, you just bought a bigger-capacity machine.

However, after considerable study, it became apparent that the problem was not in the size of the machine, but in our ability to load and unload it fast enough to get the ware back to the point where it was needed. In brief, we learned that the design of the support tables, areas, and mobile equipment was the answer. This conclusion came from studies of existing layouts, in which the machines had the capacity to wash a given number of pieces per hour, but actual counts showed that we were able to load and unload only a fraction of this amount—in some cases, only 30 percent. So even though the machine was large enough for the job, we were unable to use its full capacity.

In fact, recent research has shown that the majority of food service operations could make do with either of just two different-sized machines: a small, single-tank, or a larger, two-tank, conveyor-type machine. Each type is illustrated in the accompanying drawings and explanations. These show a standard warewasher for small to medium-sized operations and an economy "go-round" model for the larger facilities. In terms of gross-dollar yearly business, we could adopt these two basic designs and handle volumes of from $100,000 to $1 million per year. Although there are operations that exceed these figures, we know from reports that more than 90 percent of the ones in the United States fall into the dollar range that these two designs will fit.

Not only will the operator save money on the investment cost by selecting the proper machine for his volume, but he will save much in operating costs by not having a large machine that is being run at only 30 percent of capacity, wasting hot and cold water, utilities, and detergents. This is a very good example of the need to spend more time in design and equipment selection to do the job for the minimum cost.

Support Equipment

The key to efficient and fast washing is being able to feed and take away from the machine quickly. If the soiled-ware table is too small and poorly designed, there will be a pileup here and great delay in feeding the machine; if the clean-ware table is inadequate, so that there is no place to put the clean ware as it comes from the machine, we will have more delays and breaks in the operation. If you have a machine capable of washing 600 pieces per hour and you are able to sort and load and take away only 200 pieces per hour, your machine is operating at only one-third of its capacity and you are wasting a lot of effort, man-hours, and money.

Included in the support equipment must be the right number of racks to do the job, and clean-dish trucks and dollies to quickly wheel large quantities back to the point of use in just a few trips with a minimum of rehandling. For example, compartmented racks are made for washing cups and glasses; they average about 25 cups or glasses to a rack. The empty racks are usually placed on a slant shelf over the soiled-ware table, and the dirty cups and glasses are inverted into them. When one is full, it can be placed directly into the machine and the cups or glasses are washed. When they come out at the clean end, the racks can be placed onto dollies and taken back to the point of use. Because many places fail to get a sufficient number of these racks, or fail to design service stands that will take the full rack of clean glasses or cups, someone at the clean end must remove each cup and glass and put it on a tray, which is then carried to the service stand. In fact, there are many places that carry out the clean glasses by the handful, to be placed on small shelves. It doesn't take long to realize how much needless work is involved in this situation, yet you will see this done every day.

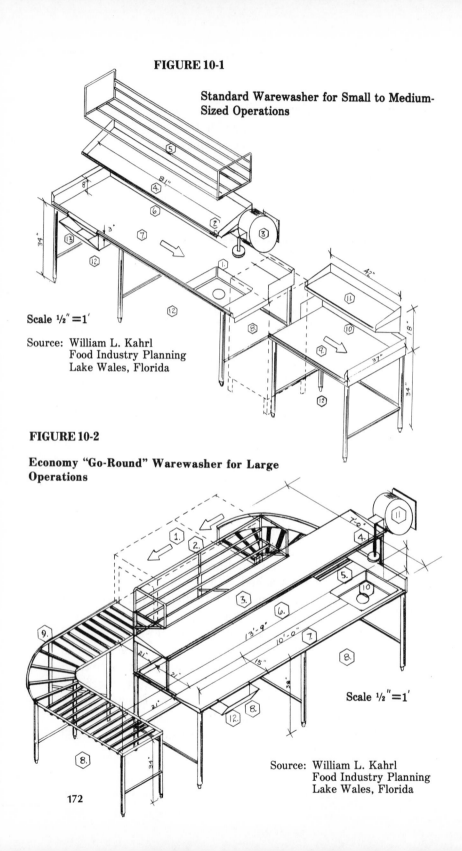

FIGURE 10-1

Standard Warewasher for Small to Medium-Sized Operations

Scale ½″ = 1′

Source: William L. Kahrl
Food Industry Planning
Lake Wales, Florida

FIGURE 10-2

Economy "Go-Round" Warewasher for Large Operations

Scale ½″ = 1′

Source: William L. Kahrl
Food Industry Planning
Lake Wales, Florida

Standard warewasher unit, designed for small to medium-sized food operations [restaurants up to $400,000/yr.]

Items

1. Standard prerinse sink, 14 ga. s/s, coved corners, 20″x22″x5″, perforated prescrap basket with three ½″ s/s rods
2. 1 drain in slant rack, pitch slant rack to this
3. Wall-mount reel rinse
4. Slant rack, wall mount, 16 ga. s/s for cup and glass racks, 16″ above table at front, 17″ above at back
5. Tubular s/s clean-rack holder, wall mount, 15″ above slant rack
6. Space for plastic flatware presoak containers
7. Soiled table, 14 ga. s/s top, s/s legs with adjustable s/s feet and braces, table pitched to prerinse sink
8. Standard (automatic) single-tank door-type machine, can be straight thru or corner
9. Clean-ware table (minimum 42″ ID length), 14 ga. s/s top, s/s legs and braces with s/s adjustable feet
10. Space for clean-flatware cylinders, sorting
11. Standard wall-mount 16 ga. s/s shelf for cylinders of clean flatware.
12. Open space under all tables for clean-dish truck, rack dollies, and refuse cans
13. Rubberized garbage scrapper*

This standard warewasher can be left-to-right or right-to-left for straight thru; can also be left-to-right or right-to-left for corner operations. Small disposer can be installed in prerinse sink if desired or permitted—1½ HP.

Garbage scrapper: garbage can [lined with plastic liner] placed under table. This rubberized garbage scrapper is hung on the edge of any dish table at any point desired. Heavy garbage is scrapped into this down to the can. This eliminates the old rubber scrapping block in the middle of the table, which made it so difficult to slide racks into the machine.

Standard warewasher unit, designed for large food service operations, with all the advantages of mechanized go-round units, but at much less cost.

Items

1. Standard single- or double-tank conveyor machine
2. Overhead s/s tubular holder for clean racks, mounted 15″ above slant shelf
3. Slant shelf for sorting cups, glasses, and bowls; 16 ga. s/s, 16″ above soiled table in front and 18″ above in rear, mounted to soiled-dish table
4. 1″ drain with s/s pipe, pitch shelf to this drain, drain into the prerinse sink
5. Conveyor rollers to machine, in integral plan recessed into table and sloped back to machine, which is 34″ high

6. Soiled-ware table, 10'-0" long OA, 36" OA depth, 38" high at set-down shelf, sloping back to 37" height at rear, 14 ga. s/s top with s/s legs and adjustable feet

7. 15" wide set-down shelf all along front

8. Spaces for refuse cans (under table), polystyrene soak tank for flatware, rack dollies, and clean-dish truck

9. Clean-ware rack return, 16 ga. s/s frame, rollers, machine conveyor pushes out racks, capacity for five racks to drain; if warewasher is in corner, this return can be wall mounted for ease of cleaning and storing under; no under pan needed—clean water can drain to a floor drain

10. Prerinse sink with perforated basket, part of soiled-dish table with drain

11. Wall-mount reel-rinse, used for prerinsing racks of dishes, washing out bus boxes and soiled trays, and cleaning down the tables

12. Garbage scrapper—same rubberized scrapper that is used on small warewasher; can be placed at any point of the table with the refuse can under; garbage can be scrapped first into this unit.

Direction for travel can be reversed if desired, although there is little difference with this arrangement. As can be seen, the operator or operators work outside the warewasher, not between the table and the machine. This enables them to unload carts, scrap, rack, load machine, and take off clean ware with very few steps. In other words, this unit has all the advantages of the much more expensive mechanized "go-round" units, at far less cost for investment and maintenance.

Eliminating Work

Every effort must be made to eliminate as much of the manual labor as possible, especially in the areas listed below.

Do Less Hand Washing. Most operations have either a dish machine or a pot-washing machine. Instead of washing everything by hand, try to utilize these machines to full advantage; after all, they represent a big investment, and the more use you can get from them the better. Because they have always been called dish machines, many think that only dishes and glasses can be washed in them. But most of the smaller trays, stainless steel pots and pans, and utensils can be washed in them as well, saving a lot of hand work, besides making this ware a lot more sterile.

Avoid Hand Carrying. There is now a great array of all kinds of mobile equipment, from fancy buscarts to simple dollies, for transporting service ware safely and quickly, with less breakage and fewer trips to the places where it is needed. I can carry about six or eight glasses in two hands, but I can move about 150 glasses at one time in racks loaded on a dolly.

Avoid Rehandling. All the parts of the operation should be carefully studied to see that there is no needless rehandling. For example, when flatware comes from the machine, it must be separated—forks, knives, spoons—and this is usually done in what are called silver boxes, most of which have four compartments. If I need spoons only, then I must remove the spoons from this four-compartmented box and carry them to the serving station. If the serving stations are equipped with silver drawers, this box is carried to the stand and each piece taken from it and placed into a compartment of the drawer—causing a lot of confusion and noise, and not helping the sanitary problem at all.

The answer is simple—sort the flatware at the clean end of the warehandling into separate containers, take them in a carrier to the station, and place the entire container in position ready for use without all that extra work.

Prevent Scorching of Pans and Utensils. Today, when we roast at lower temperatures, there is no need to have burned pans that must be scraped for hours by hand and still come out dirty. In addition, it is possible to get disposable liners, roasting bags, nonstick sprays, and even no-stick surfaces on pans that will eliminate most of this very hard and needless work. The old saying "When it's black, it's done," was very funny in cooking school, but it is no joke for the one who must try to clean the equipment.

Provide Ample Soaking Sinks. Even if the present facility is short on sinks—and most are—it is possible to buy all sizes of polyethylene or metal portable soaking sinks that can be placed where needed. This will help a great deal to loosen much of the soil and make the item easier to wash. All soiled flatware coming from the service area should be placed immediately into a soak tank with a solution of detergent and warm water to soften the food particles and make it easier to wash. When food dries on, it becomes very difficult to remove, as can often be seen by examining the tines of what are supposed to be clean forks.

Facilitate Handling Trash and Garbage. Much of the total trash and garbage ends up at the soiled end of the warehandling department. If some good system for receiving it and getting rid of it is not worked out, this could also cause a lot of work and delay, as well as an unsightly mess. Today we have all kinds of equipment and systems to solve this problem— disposing by machine, pulping, compacting, shredding, and so on. Many of these systems are considered to be too expensive, but with the new and more rigid sanitation and ecology regulations, they will become very desirable in the future.

Provide Ample Supply of All Ware. This will do more than anything else to cut down on extra steps and motions. If everyone is running around looking for a spoon, a knife, or a fork, and the man operating the warewashing machine must stop every few seconds to wash knives, then you will have a very costly operation. Some think that the less ware in service, the lower the breakage; but usually the reverse is true, because in the frantic effort to find china and glasses, more are broken.

You will see many operations with a separate storage room for a large supply of china, glassware, and flatware. It is difficult to figure why anyone would have large stocks of these supplies in a back storeroom when the dealers will carry the supplies for you. It is far better to order only what is needed and put it in service; not only is it not doing anyone much good in that back room, but you could use the space for something else, or invest the money tied up and get some interest on it.

Install Work Sinks Where Needed. Many of the small pots, pans, and utensils that are used by the cooks, for example, could be quickly rinsed for reuse rather than being thrown into the pot sinks, to be washed later. If no work sink is available, however, then the only choice is to put them in the main pot sinks. Sinks are not too expensive today, so be

sure to include enough so that the total work load can be reduced.

Limit Variety of Service Ware. This will take much of the load off not only the washing but the handling and restocking. For example, I have seen places that stock 4-, 6-, 8-, 10-, 12-, and 14-ounce glasses, when three sizes would do the job— 6-, 8-, and 12-ounce. One very fine restaurant chain has only one china plate; it is a special rectangular compartmented plate that they use for both salad and hot-food service. The less the variety you have in all kinds of ware, the easier it will be for all, including the servers.

Fortunately, many have now realized that warehandling is a very serious matter, especially with the help shortage in the industry. As with all the other departments in food service, there was no problem when help was plentiful and wages were low. If the layout, design, and equipment were not the best, we could make up for the deficiencies by simply adding more employees to overcome the problem. In a way, this was bad for the industry, because it provided no incentive to find out if we could operate more efficiently. We knew we had a problem, but we also had a very simple solution—just keep adding employees until the problem was solved. This is much the same as the problem of declining profits—it is easier to just raise prices than to expend a lot of time and effort in finding the cause for the lower profits. However, we reach a point in either situation when these simple solutions no longer work; then someone must get busy and do some thinking.

It is now possible to buy many complete warehandling systems that have been carefully designed and worked out over the years to do a much better job with far less effort and man-hours. Naturally, these complete systems cost more initially than does some inadequate system that is quickly thrown together, but over the long run, the additional investment will soon be paid back, and the benefits will continue for a long time to come. It is the same idea that was discussed about the equipment for the food service kitchen—the new efficient fryers with automatic basket lifts will seem expensive in the beginning, but if we do not have the help, the skills, or the money to pay for a lot of wasted effort, then we must turn to better and more efficient equipment.

Most industries pour back millions of dollars each year into research and development to find new equipment and ways to do a better job for less; they know that otherwise, the competition will soon put them out of business. Many are abandoning old manufacturing plants and building new ones so that they can operate more efficiently. This is not just for the sake of spending some money, but actually is a matter of survival. We in the food service industry have a long way to go, because we have been a little slow in research and development, but much progress has been made and we do have much more to work with now. However, we must be willing to realize that we need these improvements, and we must use them, or all the effort will be for naught.

SUMMARY

1. *Importance of the Function.* Consideration is finally being given to the task of warehandling today, because it has become clear that the job involves much expensive equipment and serving ware, a great deal of time and effort, the efficient functioning of all other departments, and the vitally important job of sanitation.

2. *The Warewashing Area.* The location of this area is very important, since its improper placement can vastly increase work and steps for all personnel. Modern warewashing equipment can be placed nearly anywhere, so there is no excuse for bad location.

3. *Equipment.* Many types and sizes of warewashing machines are being manufactured, but 90 percent of existing operations could use either of two models, illustrated in this chapter. Support equipment includes soiled-ware and clean-ware tables, racks, and dollies, all of which are necessary for the machines to operate at their greatest capacity.

4. *Reducing Work.* Efficiency in warehandling demands that hand washing, hand carrying, rehandling, and scorching of pans be reduced to a minimum. Soaking sinks and

work sinks should be used, a garbage-handling system set up, and an ample supply—but a limited variety—of ware provided.

QUESTIONS FOR REVIEW

1. Why is warehandling described in this chapter as "the single biggest task . . . in food service?

2. Assume that you are a server in a facility that has poorly run warehandling. What complaints might you have?

3. What factors determine the proper size of ware-washing machines for a given facility?

4. Name three types of support equipment for warehandling, and state their functions.

11

Personnel

Objectives

The greatest problem in the food service industry—that of getting and retaining the quantity and kind of help that is needed—is covered in this chapter. After studying it, the student should understand:

1. The elements and causes of the problem of hiring and keeping good employees.
2. The necessity of improving the quality of the personnel and the status of the industry.
3. The importance of hiring and training practices in helping to solve this problem.

An appropriate way to start this chapter is to reprint the lead or cover statement from an article in *Food Management Magazine*, March 1974:

HELP!
What's wrong and right with today's foodservice help?

Volumes have been written on this subject and will continue to be, especially as it concerns the food service industry, because it is a very vital and trying subject. Everyone in the food service industry, no matter what branch, asserts that the biggest problem is help, and the complaints cover a very wide range, from the shortage to being able to keep employees on the job. Once again, we will define the problems and then suggest some practical solutions for the industry.

GENERAL PROBLEMS

As in other parts of the business, there is a wide difference of opinion regarding the employee situation, and there is good reason for this. Having conducted thousands of exit interviews with employees who have quit, I can truthfully say that there are almost as many reasons for their leaving as there are resignations. In theory, it should be easy to pinpoint one or two basic reasons for this, but in actual experience, this is not possible.

Before attacking the problem, we must face the facts and realize the difficulties. It is impossible to solve anything unless the causes are known, and we have some conditions that must be recognized:

Shortage of employees, skilled and unskilled

Very high turnover of help, especially in the lower categories

One of the lowest productivity rates among industries

Low wage scale

Difficult jobs, requiring a substantial amount of physical exertion

Long hours, particularly for management

Not the best working conditions, in many cases

Difficult training task

Working hours that include nights, Saturdays, Sundays, and holidays

Many try to gloss over these facts, or hope that most of the problems facing the industry will just go away all by themselves, but it is time that we look at the whole picture just as it is, and then start to do something about it. Other industries have their employee problems as well, as evidenced by the well-publicized strikes and other difficulties that we have seen over the years. It is wise to learn early in the game that this is a continuing problem that will always exist, but it is not one that we should shy away from or try to sweep under the rug. You will hear all kinds of quickie solutions, dealing with areas such as motivation, higher pay, and company loyalty; all are important, but no one of them is the answer. Instead, we must attack from all fronts to find the answers to the problems. It is much like putting a sick food service facility back on its feet—in most cases, there is no one miracle cure that will do the job, but rather many things that must be done.

Lest you think that the employee situation in our industry has only a dark side, it should be emphasized here and now that we have made some good advances over the years, and conditions are much more in our favor. We do have better working conditions, hours have been shortened, the wage level has increased considerably, and much of the physical effort has been cut and more can be reduced in the future. Besides, we are a very large and successful industry, and predictions are that we will continue on this path.

As explained in earlier chapters, we still have a great deal to offer all levels of employment in the industry—in fact, much more than many other industries now. Perhaps we have a long way to go, but we do have a good start, and we can do much in the future to alleviate what most in the industry consider the number one problem—HELP. The most important thing to realize and learn is that the more we can aid the employees, the more the industry will benefit.

Many think this is just a one-way street—that anything given to the employees is for their benefit alone and that the company will not receive anything in return. Some of the oldsters in our business keep harking back to the good old days, when there were thousands of people looking for work at any wage and we gave them no benefits and not much consideration. When one employee left, there were three or four ready and willing to take the job. True—and once, we paid little or no taxes, and a ride on the subway cost five cents. The old days are gone, and now we must face up to what exists and do something positive about the situation.

SOLVING THE PROBLEMS

Let's set up an eleven-point program of some practical things we can and should do in the food service industry to ease the situation. No one will ever completely solve everything, but we can at least "give it a go."

Quality, Not Quantity

For too many years now, we have relied on numbers of employees, rather than a few with greater skill and productivity. Our wage scales were low in comparison to other industries, and naturally, this did not attract the better employees. Once in a whole we did find someone with ability, and he either moved up very quickly to a better position or resigned to take a better job. At one time we were known as a sort of "stopover" industry—employing people who could not find other jobs, or who were looking for some temporary employment until they could find what they really wanted. Now we are a large industry and can offer many fine jobs, excellent chances for advancement, and some rather interesting careers within our own business. This is the approach that should be taken, and then we will be able to get more competent employees in the future.

To start with, having large numbers of mediocre employees is much like having a menu with too many items—the more you have, the more problems you will encounter. The greater the number of employees, the greater the difficulties of hiring, training, supervision, and turnover. For example, the job of scheduling a large number of employees is much tougher and takes a lot more time than arranging working hours for a few. Statistics have shown that the highest amount of job turnover is in the lower brackets (those receiving the least amount of money), and although the cost of help turnover does not appear on the profit and loss statement, it is a very real and high cost over the long run. It has been estimated that it costs at least $500 to hire and train each employee, even in the lower positions (a very low figure, it would seem), and of course, as the skill required increases, so does the labor turnover expense. When one realizes that some large companies hire thousands of new employees each year, it is not hard to imagine what this turnover cost could be.

Fortunately, with all the new equipment and better systems that have been developed, we can do the same job today with far fewer employees, which means we can start shooting for more quality and less quantity. It is just a matter of simple arithmetic—if you can do the same job with 50 employees instead of 75, then you can aim for better quality. And as the skills increase, perhaps you can do the same job in the future with fewer than 50. Remember that in the chapter on serving, we pointed out that it is possible in many cases to reduce the amount of walking and effort by at least 50 percent. If we do this, then one server can take care of more customers—increasing both sales and her tips, and thus making everyone happier.

Competing on the Labor Market

When we hire someone's services in any capacity, we are in effect buying a commodity, just as though we were buying any of the product that we might use—a round of beef, or a can of string beans—and we expect full value for the money spent. When we buy that can of beans, there are certain specifications set to ensure that we will get full value, and because of this, we must expect to pay the fair market price. Most prices are determined by the law of supply and demand, as we all know, and if that can is bringing X cents, it is unlikely that we will be able to purchase it for much less. However, for years we have been trying to hire people at rates less than fair market prices, and then wondering why we have a labor problem.

Our industry has put forth great effort to be permitted exemption from the minimum wage laws set by the government, in the hope that we would be able to hire employees at a lower rate than most other industries do. On the surface, this might look like a good idea and enable us to pay less to our help, but it has not worked well. Even if we are exempt from these standards, how are we going to attract and hire good help for less than the going market figure? There are those who say that the amount of money paid is not the main consideration in keeping an employee happy. This is doubtful nowadays, but in any case, wages and salary are a most important factor in hiring. Otherwise, why do all the ads for employment stress the salary or the hourly rate? Why is the first question asked by applicants, "What is the pay?"

At the present time, we seem to be competing only with ourselves—one food service operation or company hires someone away from another, in a sort of continual swapping that in the end does not benefit the industry as a whole. We must get into a position where we can also compete with other industries on the job market, if we are to attract and hire the kind of employees we need.

Much of the current situation stems from the fact that the average person thinks ours is a business that requires little knowledge or skill, and that whatever is needed can be easily and quickly learned in a few weeks. Perhaps this was true in the past, when we were able to hire great numbers of people at low rates, and their sheer numbers made up for the lack of skill and productivity, but now that we must operate with far fewer people, we need more competent help who can and will produce more. If another industry is paying Y amount an hour for a certain job classification, we must also get into a position to pay Y amount.

Quite a few years ago, I was asked to redesign the operations of a large chain of restaurants in a foreign country, so that they could operate with about 10 percent fewer employees. Although they had no so-called wage-cost problems, the owner explained that every time a certain car manufacturer opened a new plant anywhere near one of his restaurants, the restaurant employees left to take jobs at the plant for more money. In brief, the owner of the restaurants wanted to be able to offer the same amount of money, so he could compete, hold his employees, and be able to hire competent help.

The old saying that you get only what you pay for applies to help just as much as to any other commodity. With the sophisticated systems, greater merchanization, and automation that we employ today, we do need more highly skilled labor. And there is no reason to do without it, since we are in a position to compete in the market, and we also have the future opportunities and advancement needed to hold the employees we hire.

Raising the Status

An excerpt from the report of a special task force to the Secretary of Health, Education and Welfare is reprinted here because it describes so well another of our major problems in the past:

> We must recognize that manual work has become increasingly denigrated by the upper middle class of this nation . . . . The ramifications of the low societal view of the worker are extensive and related to the personal problems of workers: low self-esteem, alcoholism, and withdrawal from community affairs. Our interviews with blue-collar workers revealed an almost overwhelming sense of inferiority: The worker cannot talk proudly to his children about his job, and many workers feel that they must apologize for their status.

Thus, the working-class home may be permeated with an atmosphere of failure—even of depressing self-degradation. This problem of esteem and identity is, perhaps, related to the recent rise in ethnic consciousness among the working class.*

This may be one of those intangible factors that most of us have never thought about, but it certainly has affected the industry—and much more than we may realize. Perhaps we in the industry are mainly responsible, because we have often looked down on most of the jobs within our business. Some of the degrading terms for these jobs—like "pot walloper," "hash slinger," "pearl diver," "bus boy," "dishwasher"—came from within our own industry before they became widespread throughout the language. As a social status symbol, even the term "waitress" or "waiter" is not too desirable and has caused many to shy away from such a position, despite the fact that these jobs have always been highly paid and, in many cases, rewarding.

As an example, a girl is proud to say she is an airline stewardess, and yet today she is doing the same thing as a waitress—serving meals and drinks—except that she does it in the air instead of on the ground. However, the airline industry from the start worked hard to give all their positions glamor, status, and very attractive uniforms. There can be little doubt that a competent waitress in a good restaurant makes far more money than a stewardess, yet, airlines have far less difficulty in hiring capable women and keeping them. Certainly a fine cook needs just as much skill, training, and experience as, say, a dental technician, but the term "dental technician" sounds better—has more of a status ring. Many people who own and operate hamburger places earn far more than the average attorney, or even some doctors, but again, in society, attorneys and doctors have higher status. So a man who owns a hugely successful hamburger business may itch to have, instead, a very posh and fancy restaurant, simply because he associates hamburgers with low status.

*Work in America, Report of a special task force to the Secretary of Health, Education and Welfare.

Now that we are an important industry, it is time to blow our horn a little more and raise our prestige to where it belongs. After all, if the food service industry stopped, there would be a lot of the upper middle class, or higher, in deep trouble. We as an industry must work on this problem and spend some time and money on a program to raise the status of both the work and the position titles. In addition, some of the job titles could be changed—"dishwasher" and "pot washer" to "warehandler," perhaps "cook" to "food server"— and we might make more use of the title "food service director." It is interesting to note now how the term "restaurant" is not being used as much any more, even by the big chains, who have come up with far different titles. Maybe this is an indication that there is a change in the wind, and it would be welcome. Shakespeare once wrote, "What's in a name?" The answer may be, more than we think.

Careful Screening

Much of the hiring in our industry has been "panic" hiring. That is, with a general shortage of help, especially in some categories, when a vacancy occurs that must be filled quickly, the tendency is to hire the first person that appears and put him to work immediately. In many instances, references are not checked—and frequently they are not even requested.

The hiring of just anyone might seem at the moment the best thing to do in a time of crisis, but very often this procedure turns out badly in the long run. We are simply borrowing time, not solving the problem of getting someone competent who will remain and become a worthwhile employee. Careful investigation before hiring does take some time, effort, and money, but it always pays off in the long run. With all the stories we hear daily about the increase in alcoholism, drug addiction, and crime, it is doubly important that we check each and every applicant as carefully as possible, since these problems are not the sole property of the applicants for the minor positions, but can be very real and damaging even at the higher levels. The trouble that can arise from hiring someone with such a problem is not just in the damage he does to himself or the position he is in; the effect can be far-reaching to others in the business, and to the very business itself.

It doesn't take long or cost much to get some references, some identification, to write a letter, or, better yet, make a phone call. Not every operation has a separate personnel section that can handle this type of job, but someone in authority can do some checking. Just letting an applicant know that you are going to check into his references, causing a slight delay in hiring, will cause many undesirables to leave and never come back.

Better Training

Some very large companies are fortunate enough to have separate training departments, but by far, most of the industry's efforts in this direction must be on-the-job training. How successful it is depends, of course, upon how capable the management and key employees are. If the people on the job haven't been trained well themselves they cannot do much to help the newcomer. The biggest problem is that most of the current employees are so busy trying to handle their own work, they have little time to stop and show someone else what to do, particularly during the rush periods. This is the reason why high labor turnover is so expensive and damaging—not only is the new employee unable to operate at a very high level of efficiency, but some skilled employee must stop his own work and help to train, so the loss is in two directions.

We must realize that some kind of training is a must. A little is better than none at all, and the program must be continuous, not a hit-and-miss affair. At one time, several of the large detergent companies would come in and train warehandlers, but some have dropped the program. The problem was that they spent hours training a crew, then came back two weeks later to check on the results and found a whole new set of employees.

Even employees who have been with a company for

some time need training—perhaps they can move up into a new job, or a new system, which is due to be installed. Management training, which is now recognized as very valuable, can go on as long as the company does.

There has been a great deal of talk about training in the food service industry—about all the schools that would be set up, the technical training that would supply all the skilled help needed—but indications are that even though we do have some of this, the bulk of the training job falls upon the individual company or operation, and it takes place on the job. Be assured, in any case, that each dollar or hour of time spent in some kind of training on a regular basis will not be lost, but will return very good dividends.

Higher Wages

The problem of higher wages in another never-ending battle for management in all industries. Such factors as increased cost of living, government regulations, more children to feed and educate, and the risk of illnesses, plus many more demands, will spur the cry for more money. Of course, there is a limit to what can be paid for certain jobs at specific times, and all businesses know very well what these are. Certainly, some programs are needed to a degree. However, none of us can just set a figure for the top amount and say that we will never pay more, because this might not hold true.

Many employers wait until the employee asks for an increase and then try to stall as long as possible. If this is the only increase system available to personnel, there will be some difficulty in keeping valuable employees. Some plan should be devised to allow for the following:

1. Merit increases, allowing for a wage increase when the employee has proved satisfactory after a given time

2. Increases for longevity, rewarding someone who is loyal and stays with the organization

3. Advancement, by which an ambitious employee

who wishes to go beyond the wage ceiling at his job level can advance to a higher position within the company

4. Bonus or profit sharing, used by many to reward people for their endeavors in making the company prosperous

5. Retirement programs and other fringe benefits, used as a reward for a job well done

In brief, there should be some built-in methods by which the employees can receive more pay or promotion without their always asking for it or threatening to leave to get what they want. Many good employees never ask for a raise, but when the time comes, they simply quit and find another job.

Along with a plan to take care of the various increases needed, we should always keep in mind the fact that *wages will go up.* This is sound thinking, and the yearly budgets and goals should be made with this fact in mind. This is why all facilities should constantly think in terms of reducing costs, increasing sales, and making more profit. An axiom in business is that a company can seldom remain in one position—it goes either up or down, and, of course, the best way is up.

Advancement and Dismissal

As explained in the preceding section, a plan for advancement should be set up by management, so that all employees know it is possible; but they should also know it will be up to them. Many people are perfectly happy with the work they are doing and do not care to move up the ladder. But if they want regular pay increases, this presents a problem, because normally, each job level does have a ceiling. In other words, employees should not expect to "sit still" and earn more and more money.

Management must also be very careful and sure before moving people up the ladder. Be certain they are ready for the next step and can handle the job, because it is almost impossible to downgrade an employee—put him in a lower position once he has advanced. Just like a company, he can't afford to go back. We see this happening all the time, particularly in management positions and other key spots. A vacancy occurs, and the company quickly picks someone without thorough investigation and moves him up, but in a short time, it becomes evident that this person was not ready for the job and cannot do it. This creates a very delicate situation for both parties—what to do next? In fact, it is much more harmful for the individual than the company, so great care must be taken in advancing as well as hiring.

Another mistake is often made when, even though the company knows a certain employee is not doing his job, they leave him in the position year after year. Then suddenly, someone comes along and notifies this person that he never did perform properly, which is most tragic. Again, it is much better for all concerned, and particularly for the individual, to change the situation just as soon as his or her inability to do the job is discovered. Certainly someone made a mistake, but it is better to correct the error as soon as possible rather than let it drag on for years.

Working Conditions

Most of us will spend almost one-third of our lives at work, and if the surroundings and conditions are not pleasant, they can produce a lot of dissatisfaction. The industry is working very hard on this, and improvements in this area will do much to help the employee situation. It might cost a little more in the beginning to provide some of the things needed to make the job more pleasant, but this cost will be almost nothing compared to the cost of losing good employees and constantly training new ones over the years.

Some of these needed items are:

Clean and adequate toilets

A decent place to eat

A place to take a break

Low noise level

Proper lighting

Good ventilation (It is difficult to work in a kitchen in temperatures as high as 120°.)

Dry, non-slip floors

Avoidance of sudden changes in temperature (running back and forth from the hot kitchen into a cold walk-in box)

Decent office space for those doing the record keeping

Dressing rooms and lockers for safekeeping of possessions

Proper tools to work with (carts for handling heavy supplies, and all the other small tools needed to perform tasks more easily)

Equipment safeguards to prevent accidents (not only provided, but explained to the people using them)

Supplies and equipment placed to reduce needless trips and steps

In addition to these physical things, there are a lot of emotional disturbances that can be avoided—shouting, confusion, arguing, needless pressures, and many more such annoyances. Just doing a job is difficult enough without adding a score of small annoyances that create poor working conditions. The better the working conditions, the better the employees will do their jobs, and this is a very important consideration.

Direct Relationship

Management and supervisory personnel must realize that employees have a variety of problems, some of which are not job-oriented but are personal. The door should always be open so that employees can at least discuss these problems, and if management can do anything at all to help, it should put forth as much effort as it can. It is always a good feeling to know that there is someone who cares about you and is willing to listen and help.

Security

Job security is also a very important consideration to most employees. It is very difficult to produce when one is constantly in fear of being fired or when one is aware that the company is not doing too well. Frankly, because of the many failures in the food service industry, there has been a lack of job security over the years that has compounded the problem of help. Even though employees may not see the profit and loss statements or know how much the sales are decreasing, they can quickly sense that something is wrong. This is one more reason why we should do everything possible to operate well and stay in good financial position at all times.

Unions

Although much of our industry is non-union, you will no doubt run into unions in certain parts of the country or in some job classifications from time to time. Where this is found today, the problems presented are not as difficult as they were many years ago. Our industry has now grown and developed to the point where we can meet union wage demands, and now have the shorter working hours in most instances and have adopted many of the fringe benefits that are required. Where there is a union to which the employees belong, it does add another factor in employee relations, but because we are not unionized on a broad national scale like the steel workers, coal miners, auto workers, etc., you are not as likely to find widespread strikes and work stoppages in the food service industry. Usually your dealings will be with a local union on a more direct basis. If your operation is successful and well-run, there should be little difficulty in setting up good cooperation with union officials.

Mid-Management

When one thinks of personnel, the emphasis is normally centered on top management or the bulk of employees in lesser positions of authority. However, just as the army has its sergeants and the navy its chiefs, we have employees at the mid-management level who are very important to the success of any operation. These are the people in jobs such as assistant managers, controllers, dining room managers, food or beverage managers, heads of a department, and so on. These people actually oversee the day to day operation and try to satisfy the guests' needs. This group is the link between management and the bulk of the employees and they see that company policy is followed and enforced. Because most of our training is "on the job," it is mid-management that assumes most of this burden from day to day.

The most brilliant top management, policies, and systems won't go far if mid-management is weak, as has been learned time after time by so many who have failed in food service. Our business covers long operating hours, Saturdays, Sundays, and holidays with many details that must be constantly checked by mid-management personnel, for no manager or vice president can supply all the direction needed for success.

Having studied so many operations over the years, it is easy to spot the operation that lacks strong key employees; it is usually in difficulty and the manager is confused and harried because he lacks strong support. For example, when one has an excellent dining room manager, there is no need to worry whether the guests are being served well and fast—a good food service manager will be out there at meal times seeing that the food is prepared and served right. The best manager won't succeed if he or she doesn't have strong people in key mid-management positions—it is team work that produces results!

The employees are the heart of the organization—the success of the venture depends largely on whether or not they do a good job. A dedicated and highly skilled crew can operate any type of facility and make it go, but a poor set of employees will not be able to make a success of even the best operation that can be planned and devised.

You will take many other courses concerning motivation and psychology, all of which will help a great deal in your dealings with your fellow workers and employees. In this text, we have listed a few of the practical factors that can help— things learned from many years of actual experience in dealing with employees in the food service industry. There is no one magic solution to the problem, but there are many things that can be done to help, and the best course is to do as much to improve as possible. The one minor factor you deem unimportant might be just the thing that will cause you the most trouble. Remember that you are dealing with people, and people can be very complex.

SUMMARY

1. *Labor Problems.* Hiring and keeping good employees is hard to do in most industries; in food service, the problem is compounded by high turnover, low productivity, a relatively low wage scale, long and inconvenient working hours, difficulty of training, and working conditions that are frequently below standard.

2. *Solutions.* Given the current shortage of help, the industry must strive to acquire employees with higher skills, by thorough screening of applicants and careful training of those hired. In order to compete on the job market, it must offer higher wage levels, raise its own and employees' status, provide for pay increases, advancement, and fringe benefits, and furnish better working conditions, interpersonal relationships, and job security.

3. *Improvement.* The labor situation in the food service industry has been improving somewhat in recent years, owing partly to increases in the sophistication of systems,

mechanization, and automation. If management continues to make reasonable efforts to solve the other problems, they should be greatly lessened in the future.

QUESTIONS FOR REVIEW

1. Name some of the underlying causes of the labor problem in the food service industry.

2. What are the reasons for the industry's current need for more highly skilled employees?

3. Under what circumstances should wage increases or other additions to pay be given?

4. Describe in some detail the features you would include in the plans for a new facility, for the purpose of providing good working conditions for employees.

12

Sanitation and Safety

Objectives

These two subjects, once largely disregarded, have now become prominent in the food service industry. When he has finished this chapter, the student should be able to state:

1. The reasons for the importance of sanitation in the industry.
2. Possible dangers from lack of good sanitation, and ways to help eliminate them.
3. Methods for improving safety and reducing accidents for employees and customers.

The reason for grouping these two topics together—the two S's—is that they have been slighted too often in the past. Both these functions are so easy to forget and skim over that a lot of activity has emerged from many sources recently regarding the fact that our industry is not paying enough attention to them.

In one large city, conditions became so bad that one of the local television stations joined with the local health officials and actually visited public eating places of all kinds. Where they were permitted to enter, they took pictures of conditions and showed them on the air. Many were not pleasant to view, and a lot of public interest was created. In other sections of the country, health departments are getting more backing and can now enforce the sanitation codes with stiff fines, and even closings, to assist in the much-needed cleanup. One city has even considered forcing public eating places to put in windows where the public, if they choose, can go to see what the "back of the house" looks like. This is not a bad idea; some of the kitchens I have seen would need frosted glass to stay in business.

Another interesting fact being learned is that there seems to be no direct relationship between the reputation; degree of elegance, or high prices of the place and its cleanliness. Some very well-known restaurants were exposed, which was quite a shock to many people. Obviously, everyone in the industry must pay more attention to sanitation in the future, because failure to do so can be very damaging to the business and the pocketbook.

PROBLEMS IN SANITATION

Our main difficulty with sanitation is that the industry is growing so fast and needs so many new employees each year that it is hard just to keep up with the serving of food, let alone take care of these other jobs. Another problem is that even though we do have some new food service facilities, most are old, badly worn, and very hard to keep clean. These were designed in the days when help was very plentiful—when food facilities had large cleaning crews that came in each night and cleaned the entire place completely, from one end to the other. Now that help is short and we cannot afford all these employees, the job of cleaning has become very difficult. Most operations take care of the business of serving first and leave the cleanup to last.

SOLVING THE PROBLEMS

Cleanliness Is a Must

The first and most important thing to learn about proper sanitation is that the place should be clean at all times, not just before the supervisor comes to check, or the health inspector visits. If your operation could not be shown to anyone at any time, you are not doing a good job of sanitation or cleaning. If the floors are covered with litter, the trash cans overflowing, equipment not clean, pots and pans piled high in the sinks, food and supplies not in place, then it is time to do something about the sanitation. Once a customer gets very bad service, even though it is good most of the time, he will probably not return; in the same way, all the excuses in the world won't change someone's mind about the cleanliness of an establishment once he has seen it dirty.

Cleanliness is an "all-the-time" affair that we must recognize and live with. The signs posted in so many places, CLEAN AS YOU GO, mean exactly what they say—proper cleaning is something that goes on every minute and hour that you are in operation, not something that is done each night, or once a week.

The first step in solving this problem is for management to learn this and really believe in it. If management is lax and does not insist on good clean work habits among the employees, then poor conditions will exist. All employees must be thoroughly indoctrinated into this practice from their first day. If we all learn from the start that we should try to avoid making messes, and that if we make them, they must be cleaned up at once, most of the problem will be solved.

There is an old Dutch saying, "Many hands make light work," and this certainly applies to cleaning. Each employee must be taught to take pride in his or her station and to keep it clean and neat at all times. This idea can be contagious: If a new employee starts work in a place that is clean and kept clean all the time, he will soon fall into the same habit, but if he begins work in a dirty messy operation, it won't be long before he falls into a similar lax pattern. It may require some extra effort at first, and quite a bit of checking, but once the idea has been firmly implanted, the whole job will be much easier.

Rules and Regulations

All levels of government—city, county, state, and federal—have their sanitary codes and regulations. Many consider these to be rather severe or "nit-picking," but they have been set up for a very good reason. We are dealing with a product that is consumed by human beings, so there can't be too much care taken in its handling and serving. If a new pair of shoes pinches your feet, you can return them, but bad food could make you very ill and have serious consequences.

Therefore, regardless of your personal feelings about some of them, you must abide by all these regulations. They have been developed over the years and are just as much of a protection for you as they are for others. There are valid reasons for forbidding smoking in food-serving areas and for enforcing washing of hands after leaving toilets. Proper temperatures for storing, handling, preparing, and serving foods might not seem important, but a serious outbreak of food poisoning will be quite another matter.

Learn early in the game to cooperate fully with all

authorities and follow the rules; it will not only save you a lot of headaches and grief, but will benefit you in the long run. If there are rules that you think need changing, go through your local association or other channels to change them in an orderly fashion, but don't start a one-man crusade of defiance on your own. It is much better to be safe than sorry.

Tools and Equipment

Another big step forward would be to see that your employees have the right equipment and tools to do the job correctly, all the way from large pieces of equipment down to clean cloths for properly wiping table tops.

Today, we can build into our plans much better sanitation from the start, with a number of ideas:

Smaller areas—less to clean

Less major equipment—fewer pieces

More mobile equipment—everything put on wheels (except equipment hooked up to water and drains), making the job much easier

Materials and equipment that is either self-cleaning or easier to clean—equipment surfaces, walls, floors, ceilings, etc.

Automatic washing machines of all types—for ware, pots and pans, even portable pressure-cleaning units that can speed and facilitate the work

The right number of sinks of all kinds, located where they are needed

A place for everything, to keep items where and when they are needed

Temperature controls for all food handling, plus indicators that will constantly inform whether the correct temperature is being maintained

Automatic scrubbing and drying machines for floors,

vacuum machines for rugs, sweeping machines, and many more new pieces of equipment that can take much of the manual labor and drudgery out of this job and do it better and faster

In addition, you should also check to see that all the small things needed for proper housekeeping are available—enough clean mops hanging where they are needed, a sink in which to rinse and wash the mops, clean cloths to wipe up as the work progresses, enough trash cans located where they are needed, a small hand sweeper for a quick brushup of the carpet between meals, pickup pans and small brooms for spills or littering, proper soaps and detergents, good mop buckets, scrapers for grills—in other words, a whole list of seemingly minor items that your employees need at all times to do a good continuous job of cleaning.

The fact that these are not, in fact, minor items can be easily illustrated. Many of the places I visit complain about their floors being slippery, even though they are made of special nonslip materials. The problem is improper cleaning. With all the grease in kitchens, it is impossible to thoroughly clean any floor with a dirty mop and a small bucket of water, the method used in many places. With this procedure, about all you are doing is spreading the dirt and grease around, not removing it, and this will eventually result in a heavy buildup of slippery film that will cause trouble. We must scrub or mop correctly and then rinse away this dirt, to have clean and non-slip floors.

Outside Help

Because of the shortage of skilled food servers, the less cleaning they must do, the more time they can devote to what they were hired for—the proper serving of food. One thing that can be done immediately is to get all the outside help possible, especially with the large cleaning jobs that are so difficult—rug shampooing, window cleaning, lawn care, washing the roof, cleaning exhaust ducts, and many more.

Many will say that they cannot afford these services,

but here again, it would pay to at least investigate. Most of the service firms are better equipped than the facilities are to do these jobs—they have the right tools, and their employees are trained in one specific job, such as bug and rodent extermination. At least get the prices for these services, and then figure whether or not your own employees can do as good a job for the same money. In addition to the actual cash comparison, realize also that the more time your skilled food servers spend on cleaning and other nonproductive jobs, the less time they will have to perform the jobs they were hired to do. When a cook has put in a very busy day preparing food, he is not in the mood to spend additional time doing heavy cleaning jobs. Many think they can do a better job themselves, but I have seen a lot of ruined carpeting caused by someone's efforts to do it himself without knowing how.

Less Food Preparation

Another practical way to get relief from the cleaning chore is to cut down on food preparation as much as possible. As was said before, we are in the food service business, not manufacturing. You will learn that most of the dirt, garbage, and other tough cleanup jobs are in the food-preparation area, not food service. Also, the equipment used in food preparation is much larger, more complex, and harder to clean.

Let's take one item as an example: Assume that you are planning to produce all your own potato items from scratch, including mashed and french fries. First there is the job of receiving and storing large bags of potatoes, which are rather dirty to start with. Then comes the peeling in a peeler and the eyeing of the potatoes. For mashed, the potatoes must then be cut up, boiled on a range in a kettle, put into a mixer, and whipped; for french fries, they must be cut through a machine and then be blanched and put into pans ready for frying. Think of all this mess—the bags, the peelings, the equipment that needs to be cleaned, all the pots and pans used. Contrast this to buying frozen blanched french fries that are ready to be placed in the fryer for immediate service, or instant whipped potatoes that can be quickly prepared right in the pan they will be served from, again for instant service. And when you are figuring the end cost of those frozen french fries as against the whole-potato cost, don't forget to add in the preparation-labor cost and, what is more important, the cleanup cost.

You can analyze many more jobs that you are doing, to see where the load can be reduced. The more cleaning we can eliminate and avoid, the easier the job will be for all.

Summary of Sanitation

1. Good housekeeping and cleanliness are a must in the food service industry.

2. You must abide by all the rules and regulations set forth—in fact, it would be better to go a step further, if possible.

3. Food service facilities must be clean at all times, not just once in a whole.

4. It is not as difficult a job as many make it. With the equipment and systems available today, the chance to get outside help, reduction of preparation, and proper training of the employees and management, it is possible to have a clean place all the time with far less effort than was needed years ago.

5. Remember to *CLEAN AS YOU GO!*

SAFETY

The problem of safety in the food service industry has come to the fore recently, receiving a lot of attention from all sides—the operators, the public, and the authorities. In one geographical area, for instance, all new plans must be examined and checked before they can be approved for building, to see that proper safety precautions have been taken. Once again, the shortage of help may be partly responsible; it has probably caused a rise in the accident rate, because not only

do the employees today work under more pressure, but they are asked to perform a variety of jobs and handle many different kinds of equipment. These two factors tend to increase the chances for accidents.

Regulations and Insurance

One of the main reasons so many in the industry have failed to comply with safety regulations or to think much about the consequences is that they have insurance against accidents, fire, and so on, and figure that the insurance companies or workmen's compensation will handle all the claims at no cost to them. They feel that if there is a fire (and we have many of them) due to faulty exhaust systems or lack of automatic sprinklers, the insurance will pay for the damage and nothing will be lost.

However, someone could be seriously hurt or killed in that fire, for one thing. Also, it might take months to rebuild and try to recapture the business, and then, more than likely, the insurance rate would be increased. If you have a series of accidents to the public—falls, say, or foreign objects in the food—your public-liability insurance will cover these, but each time this happens, again your insurance rate will increase. In brief, you are paying for bad safety conditions, whether or not you realize it.

The often-used expression, "Safety is no accident," is true. All of us can install and maintain most of the safety features needed, and we can do it at a price we can afford. At the time we are installing these things, the price might seem a bit high, but if we don't do it, the cost later could be much higher. For example, we all know that many of the fires in food facilities are started in exhaust systems, where ducts are grease-laden; either there are no grease filters in the hoods or they are completely worn out, or there are no automatic extinguishing systems. Problems could be avoided by spending a little more to put in the right kind of equipment: hoods that are almost self-cleaning, filters that can be washed easily and filter out most of the grease, chemical extinguishing systems that will quickly put out a fire before it can do much damage. Trying to get by with old, worn-out equipment that is dangerous to handle and does not have the proper safety features might look like economy, but in the long run, it could cost much more than the price of a new piece.

It is easy to get professional advice in this area, because most insurance companies have special departments that spend all their time trying to keep industrial accidents down. They would be happy to send in a trained person, at no cost to you, to examine your facility and point out the areas where changes should be made. Many in our industry are reluctant to bring in outsiders like this, or representatives of the health department, who can also help you with your sanitation problems. This attitude is hard to understand, when the service is free and could benefit the facility a great deal. We should not be afraid or embarrassed to ask for help in any part of our business; it does not indicate that management does not know what it is doing, but that it is progressive and wants to improve and expand.

Accidents to Employees

According to statistics gathered over the years, the majority of accidents to employees fall into four categories:

Burns

Falls

Cuts

Colds and flu

These accidents can be minor in nature or very serious. In any event, they are costly, particularly if the employees are in top positions, because the loss of time and productivity can really be damaging when help is so short.

Burns. These are common in our business, because of the constant handling of hot foods and equipment. Many burns can be traced to faulty equipment—for instance, containers that are too large and bulky to handle, ovens that are old and difficult to load and unload. Many, however, are traceable to such simple causes as a lack of heat pads or gloves readily available for handling these hot items. Steam and hot-fat burns can be very serious and painful, because the temperatures involved are so high and the degree of burn likely to be so much greater. The prevention for this type of accident lies in proper training, as well as in having the right equipment, since new, inexperienced employees are much more apt to receive this type of injury until they learn just how to handle themselves in the kitchen.

Falls. This type of accident, also very common in our industry, can result in very serious injury. Falls can be traced to a number of factors—slippery and wet floors, objects on the floor to stumble over, trying to carry too much at one time, hurrying around under pressure. It has been proved that if the proper precautions are taken, this type of accident can be greatly reduced. That clean-as-you-go idea can be of great help here; one pat of butter dropped on the floor can be a very serious hazard if not picked up at once.

Cuts. These have been very prevalent in our business, because of the great amount of knife work and use of chopping and slicing machines that were not properly designed. Once again, the frequency depends on the skill of the employee using the knife or the slicer, and since we must hire and train so many new employees each year, the danger still exists. However, once again, the less food-preparation work we do, the less knife work there will be and, of course, the fewer of these mishaps. If we eliminate most of the meat cutting and provide many of the newer and better-designed machines now available, many of these jobs can be reduced and the safety records improved.

For example, it was once routine that each afternoon, one of the servers was assigned the job of cutting hundreds of lemon wedges. This can be a difficult job for a novice, and many times cuts were sustained. Now we have a very simple hand-operated machine that cuts a whole lemon into sections, safely and in about one-fourth of the time. Another difficult knife job was the slicing of tomatoes; if the knife was dull, the chance of cuts was much greater. Here again, we can buy a simple machine that safely cuts the whole tomato into slices, saving time and a lot of cuts.

It is important to remember that a knife is a dangerous tool in the hands of someone inexperienced, so it is important to analyze all these jobs and eliminate the amount of knife work as much as possible. As for those new slicing, chopping, grinding, and dicing machines, make sure they have the correct guards and that employees using them are thoroughly and carefully instructed in their proper use and handling.

Colds and flu. This might seem to be a very strange category, but we do have a high rating in this department. The high incidence is caused by extreme changes in temperatures—from air-conditioned dining rooms in and out of very hot kitchens, or constant trips from hot kitchens into refrigerators or freezers.

With proper design, we can now reduce this hazard a great deal. Although dining areas still might be cool, there is no need for extremely hot kitchens now, because of better exhaust systems and easier ways of cooling these areas to a more livable temperature. I have seen kitchens as hot as 125°, and this does not make for very pleasant working conditions. We have also learned to design equipment better, providing more insulation and better use of the heat so that more of it goes into the cooking of the product rather than into the cook's face.

Earlier in the book it was mentioned that walk-in coolers and freezers are meant for bulk storage, not as workboxes. If the cook must constantly run in and out of these while working, not only is he subject to catching cold, but he is also wasting a lot of time and steps. Workboxes should be the reach-in type, located conveniently in the work area—then it becomes a matter of opening a door or drawer to quickly get the product needed.

It is always the little thing that no one notices or corrects that causes accidents—the door that swings out into a busy aisle; the use of one door for both in and out, with no glass window so people can see if someone is coming the other way; the empty glass rack that is left on the floor for someone to trip over because no space has been created for empty racks; a long pot handle left sticking out into the aisle when the pot is on the range, instead of being turned back so no one can run into it. Also, many accidents are caused by one person's trying to do a job meant for two. Lifting and removing a heavy garbage can, or lifting and pouring 50 pounds of hot fat, requires the effort of two people.

Accidents to Customers

We must also consider safety for our customers—in fact, more lawsuits and costs can come from this direction than from the employees. It is surprising to discover the number of public accidents in our business and their causes—an old chair finally collapses and the guest has a serious fall; just one step up or down is not properly lighted or indicated, causing a great number of falls; mats are not recessed and provide a stumbling block; exit doors open directly into a driveway; concrete ties for parking spaces are constantly being tripped over by guests; glass and other foreign objects are found in the food; burns occur from hot beverages being spilled.

Each time an accident does happen and a guest is involved, a report must be made at once for the insurance company, and it would pay management to study these reports. More than likely, if there are a number of repeats, the insurance company will notify you of them and of the corrective action needed. If there are a number of cases where food and beverages are spilled on guests, it could be that either the servers are not well trained or the service aisles are too small and the tables too close together. If several people fall down that one set of steps, immediate action should be taken to correct the situation. Most of the corrections needed for better safety are minor things that do not require a great deal of time or money, but they do require immediate attention, because the next accident could be a very serious one, resulting in great damage and cost.

SUMMARY

1. *Sanitation Problems.* The publicity currently being given to sanitation has focused attention on this subject, so that, more than ever, steps must be taken to ensure cleanli-

ness. A dirty or unsanitary food service operation not only can be fined or even closed for infraction of government regulations, it can be the cause of severe illness for employees and customers. The problem is made more acute by the help shortage and the difficulty of cleaning old and worn facilities.

2. *Solutions.* Public eating places must be clean at all times, so personnel must be trained to "clean as you go." Management should abide by all government codes, provide proper tools and equipment for cleaning, hire outside help for the big jobs, eliminate as much as possible of the food preparation, and, above all, emphasize that cleanliness is a must.

3. *Safety for Employees.* The most common accidents that befall food service workers are falls, burns, cuts, and colds and flu. Even though a business is covered by accident insurance, such mishaps can have serious consequences and must be reduced. Employee training, precautions against falls, use of modern equipment, and moderation of kitchen temperatures can all help reduce accidents and illness. A proper exhaust system and automatic sprinklers will decrease fire hazards. Insurance companies and government agencies will provide free inspections to locate possible danger spots.

4. *Safety for Customers.* Accidents to customers can be costly in damage, money, and business. Attention to detail is vital in eliminating causes of accidents, and great care must be taken in the matter of purity of the food that is served.

QUESTIONS FOR REVIEW

1. What factors cause difficulty in maintaining good sanitation in the food service industry?

2. When should cleaning be done in the food-preparation area?

3. What are some of the ideas that can be built into a new facility to aid in sanitation? in safety?

4. Assume that you are making an apple pie from scratch. List the equipment and utensils that would have to be cleaned when the job was done.

5. For the next few weeks, watch your local newspaper for reports concerning sanitation and/or safety in public eating places, and relate any you find to information given in this chapter.

13

Forecasting and Guidelines

Objectives

The success of a food service operation depends very greatly on management's knowledge regarding the facility's day-to-day financial well-being, as this chapter shows. After completing it, the student should be able to:

1. Understand the relation of guideline figures to successful operation.
2. Name several types of figures that management should keep in order to adjust the operation.
3. Know how to anticipate changes in business for purposes of forecasting.

We are using the terms *forecasting* and *guidelines* here to encompass the areas now called *accounting* and *budgets*. Just as we separated food preparation from food service, we need to make some distinctions in this area.

DEFINITION

The dictionary defines *accounting* as, "in bookkeeping, a statement of money transactions, or of assets and liabilities, of a person or business."

Strictly speaking, accounting by itself is meant either to tell what happened to the past or to give a financial picture as of a certain time. In simple terms, the profit and loss statement gives you the former information, and the balance sheet the latter. Naturally, all businesses must have these reports for a number of reasons, but if any business or industry is to be successful, it needs much more information than this. It must know what it is doing and forecast what it will be doing, as well as state what it did previously. Finding out the results for a month that has passed is important, but the information is usually late in coming and does not afford the chance to make the quick adjustments needed to keep on course or within the budget.

Another broad difference between accounting and the type of controls we will be studying in this chapter is that the accounting work can be carried out away from the operation, as when figures are sent to some office or central point where they are accumulated in advance of the statements. Most of the controls explained in this text can be gathered and figured

on the premises for immediate use. It is very important that management on the spot take a more active part in finding out what is happening in many areas, so that quick action can be taken to adjust the parts of the operation that are out of line.

Fortunately, we now have many new systems and electronic aids that can give this information right at the operation, while taking less of management's time than do many of the older accounting systems. For example, inventory-taking time and effort can be reduced by at least 75 percent; the old task of auditing and matching guests, which once took many hours of work, can now be done in minutes by computer registers; sales counts can be obtained in a matter of minutes now, as against the long, expensive routine used before. All these new systems have been developed because we need more information faster but don't want to burden management with more hours spent at a desk trying to do long and laborious computations; in fact, we want management to spend *less* time on this job, so it can give more time to supervising the service and serving of the food.

Not only is much of the information being presented by accounting to management too late in coming, but many of the reports are never even read or used. It is much like taking a trip in a car: First the destination is set, then a map is obtained to show the course; and on the trip, there are seen all sorts of "guides"—route numbers, signs that warn of curves, signals, railroad crossings, intersections, and so on. The good driver will not only follow the route as indicated on the map; he will also read and pay attention to all the advance warning signs in order to have a successful trip. This is what we must do in the food service industry—stop operating on guesses, whims, and personal opinions, and follow statistics. The crystal ball might be all right for a fortune teller, but we need more accurate information to be successful.

First of all, we need daily and weekly figures of various kinds to know exactly what and how we are doing. These are the warning or directional signs by which we can make immediate adjustments that keep us on course. Constant review and study of these figures will let us know quickly just how the business is going, so we should pay attention to them and act accordingly. If the daily sales figures or meal counts are showing a decrease in business, action should be taken. In such a case, some investigation is called for to try to find out why this is happening; it is not enough to just sit by and assume that everything is going well and that the sales will increase in the future. It could be that something has happened in your service and serving departments to slow service, or perhaps a new operation has opened nearby that is taking some of the business, which means you must adjust quickly to the new volume of business or find ways to recapture those lost customers.

Then, we must have forecasting, or some realistic idea of what lies ahead. This is the information that enables us to set the course for the future and keep the business under control. This information could be the prediction for the next day, week, month, or year—or, better yet, it could cover all the periods. It could comprise a wide range in anticipation of what is coming—seasonal business, influx of tourists, special events, holidays, vacation times at schools and colleges, the addition of more rooms and beds to a hospital, forecasts of general business trends in the industry or the nation, and so on. In other words, good management must not only know what is happening, but have a good idea of future business as well, and this should be based on some facts and figures rather than on pure guesswork.

The good manager can tell you just when business will decline each year, how long the decline will last, and when it will start to increase again. If he waits until the third or fourth week of the decline to reduce payrolls and other expenses, there will naturally be a loss for this period. By the same token, if he fails to get ready for the increase in business that he knows from past experience is coming, he will lose a lot of sales until he can get the facility into high gear again. The adjusting of a business either up or down should be made in advance; you can't rush out after the busy season has started and find a number of trained and skilled employees in one day, but you could have been gradually adding to the force in advance to be ready.

DEPARTMENTS AFFECTED

Once you have lost the money or the customer in the food service industry, it is very difficult to recoup either. Not only will good advance information enable you to get the maximum sales, but it will enable an operation to reduce waste of all kinds, and this is very important, since many departments are affected by it.

Purchasing

Many operations seem to go along throughout the year buying just about the same amounts with each purchase, but actually we know that the amounts of food, beverages, and supplies should be closely tied to the sales and the needs. When we know when the sales will increase or decline, it is a simple matter to adjust the purchases in advance, to avoid having either not enough to take care of the business, or too much, which will result in inventories that are too large and costly as far as waste and pilferage are concerned.

Work Force

Our work force must also be kept in line with the amount of business done, and unfortunately, the number of employees is not something that can be suddenly turned off and on like a water faucet. Advance knowledge that we will need more employees means that the force can be built up gradually to meet the demand; the same records will tell you when fewer man-hours will be needed. This cutback can very often be done very easily, because of the high turnover in the business anyway. For various reasons, employees quit and leave, and if this happens in advance of the slowdown period, the employee who leaves need not be replaced, because you know that he or she will not be needed in a short while.

Food Preparation

The same prediction figures should be used very carefully to control food production. Again, based on actual figures, you should know every day how much to prepare. An article in a recent magazine pointed out the fact that most of the waste of food in institutional feeding results from a lack of correct portioning and not knowing how much to prepare. Even with good prediction figures, you will not always be right in determining the amounts to be made each day, but in the long run you will save a lot of food or, even worse, run-outs, by controlling production. Food can be expensive, and it does not take too many wasted orders going into the garbage cans each day to add up to a sizable figure at the end of the year.

In most operations, the amount to be prepared each day is left up to the cooks. But when we realize that few of these people ever see the sales or customer counts, how can we expect them to know how much to prepare? Because they know they are only guessing, very often they make more than is needed, just to make sure the item will not run out. Management must control production from forecasts, or at least see that the food-production manager has the information needed.

Menus and Merchandising

These too must often be changed because of anticipated events. The menu can be changed and balanced to match either a reduced or an increased work force, or to better suit the type of clientele at various times of the year. If predictions are that food prices will increase, or that even one or two items will be in short supply, the menu can be adjusted to take care of this situation. In the chapter on merchandising, it was clearly stated that the menu must be constructed so that it can be changed and adjusted easily and quickly, and these are a few more reasons why.

Budgeting

In the past, it was frequently the custom to set certain percentages in advance for items like food cost, wage cost, and so on, and insist that management maintain these figures constantly. This practice caused a great deal of confusion. People who know food service operating know that it is impossible to set one figure and reach it each month of the year. Business normally fluctuates, and so should the budget figures.

In fact, many in the business do not actually know what they themselves should be attaining, but rather base their operation on what others are achieving. Every so often, reports come out indicating that the national average for wage costs is, say 30 percent, and right away, many people latch onto this figure and set it as the goal for their operations. Not only do they select it as the year-end target, but they insist that the manager hit this figure each week and month of the year, which is not possible. The expense figures you can attain depend on a lot of different factors—your organization, prices, volume of business, physical plant and layout, menu, and many others. It may be that with the perfect combination, you should be operating with a 20 percent figure; on the other hand, with a bad setup, you might be lucky to hit 40 percent. Then, too, during those three weeks when your business is off each year, the budget figures must be upped to cover the lack of business; when you hit the peak, the figures can be lowered. However, at the end of the year, you should come out with an average figure that is desirable.

Quickly picking figures out of the air for a budget can be very dangerous and harmful, because you could be setting goals that are impossible to reach, or you could be doing better than the expense set. When the budget figures are more in line with the business done, management has a chance to adjust and get ready for what is coming.

MARKET, TRENDS, PRICES

Advance knowledge of these factors will also help anyone in our business to do a better job. There are many sources supplying this information—daily papers, trade magazines, associations, and even your suppliers can keep you advised of what will happen regarding many of the items you will use. Naturally, not all the predictions will be 100 percent accurate, but in general, it pays to have some idea of what is in the wind. This explains in part why so many food establishments have tried portion cutting or reducing quality, both of which can be very harmful to the business—they did not anticipate price increases, and when losses started to appear, the quick solution was to cut size and quality. It would be better to raise the price or, if the price can not be raised, to drop the item from the menu.

TYPICAL GUIDELINE FIGURES

Now we can list most of the guideline figures needed to make these reports, and supply the information needed for proper control. None of these figures are new to the industry, but they are used in varying degrees in the various segments.

Many managers do not have the staff or, more important now, the equipment needed to get these figures, which is unfortunate, because the more of these we can get and use, the better the operations will do in all respects. Because of the great lack of statistics and information like this in the food service industry, we have very few realistic guides that can be applied to the same type of operations. For example, just how many school lunches should be served in an efficient operation per man-hour? What should be the top dollar sales per hour for a certain size of fast-food operation? If we had more information like this, it would be possible to establish standards that anyone could use to correctly measure his own place. The lack of this factual information has hurt from two directions—we are not making the money we should or are trying to hit goals that are impossible to reach.

Dollar or Meal Sales

This figure must be tallied, usually by the meal, shift, or day, and a total per-week figure kept. Most operations keep a running record of sales available for checking by management. Some run comparisons for the previous week, or the same week a year ago, and indicate whether sales are up or down.

Weekly Food Costs

This can be shown as a dollar amount for the food used or can be expressed as a percentage of sales—or per meal, in the case of institutions not dealing in cash. This figure should be determined at least once each week; some operations figure a daily cost, which is much better but involves more work. Many work under the complete monthly inventory system for arriving at costs, so, of course, they get this figure only once a month, and then it usually takes about ten to fifteen days to figure the actual cost. In other words, they would not know until October 10 or 15 what their food cost was for the month of September. By that time it is too late to make any adjustments must get the important control figures frequently, in order to make the corrections needed and keep the operation in balance.

Weekly Wage Costs

Normally, these are figures each week for most places, because the payroll is on a weekly basis. However, should the pay period be two weeks, it would be advisable to figure the wage cost each week anyway, for the benefit of management and control. This is usually stated as either a percentage of the dollar sales or per meal, whichever is the case, and is much easier to compute than the food cost.

Hourly Sales

Not many operations compute or use this figure, but it can be a most useful guideline in controlling operations. Since most facilities have some kind of register for recording sales or meals, it is a simple matter to take a reading each hour and record the figures at the end of the day. They will tell you exactly when you are and are not doing business, and not only what the peak hour is, but exactly how much you do during that period of time. Many who have tried this procedure have found that they had many very slow hours of the day or night, and have been able to shorten hours of operation to help the financial picture. It is not enough just to know that you do X dollars for the total dinner period, which could last for four hours; perhaps you will discover that most of this activity is in the last two hours, which means you could delay the start of food production, thus serving fresher food, and perhaps use fewer employees at the beginning of the period and more later when they are needed.

These figures will also tell you what your peak or top capacity is for one hour. You might find out that it is not high enough, and work on the speed of service to increase the figure. If you find out most of the business is coming within a very short space of time, then you had better concentrate on that hour to serve as fast as possible and realize maximum sales.

Item Sales Counts

Few operations have very complete or accurate records on the amounts of each item sold, because computing this by hand with marks on a menu or piece of paper is quite a job and takes a lot of time. However, this is a very vital figure, and can be used in so many ways by management that accurate records should be kept. We do not need counts on all items; tomato juice, coffee, tea, and many of the smaller items can be left out, but certainly there should be records on the sales of the main items, particularly those that require preparation or production. This figure can be used as a guide in purchasing, spot-checking pilferage, determining the amount of food to be produced, indicating what items can be dropped from the menu because they are not selling—in fact, it is difficult for me to see how anyone could run a food operation very efficiently without these sales counts.

Fortunately, all operations today can obtain computerized register systems that automatically tally sales of all key items, so that management has an instant count of them after each meal. This is the same type of system that pre-rings checks, controls food and beverages being served, and extends and adds checks, yet there are those who say they cannot afford such a system. Just getting the sales-tally figure on items each day would pay for the machine, not to mention all the other savings involved.

Sales or Meals per Man-Hour

Some food operations have used this figure for years, particularly chains having several or more like units. This is the figure that shows the efficiency of the operation. Once again, it is not enough to rely solely on the labor-cost percentage figure.

It is an easy figure to compute each week. You will have either the total dollar sales or meals served, and your payroll hours must be recorded, so total hours on the payroll sheet for all employees, divided into the sales, will give you either the dollar sales per man-hour or meals per man-hour. If you and I have like operations and I am producing $8 per man-hour and you are producing only $6 per man-hour, it is very obvious that I am operating more efficiently than you are. The same would apply to meals per man-hour; if one school is serving 30 meals and another only 15, something is wrong. You as a manager can also make good use of this figure to check yourself from week to week. If you are doing that $8 per man-hour one week and suddenly drop to $6 the next, it is time to do some investigating to find out why.

It is unfortunate that not many operations make use of this very valuable figure, because if they did, we could better compare efficiency of operations in like groups. For example, if you knew from a large group of reports that the proper production figure for a school-lunch feeding program was X meals per man-hour, and you were only producing half that amount, the immediate conclusion would be that you were not doing a very good job. This is the figure that measures your productivity.

Inventory Turnover

Excessive inventories, particularly in the food service industry, are not good or advisable. We are dealing with a perishable product, or, at best, one with a short shelf life. The longer you keep the same item, the more chance there will be for waste, spoilage, and shrinkage, which cost money. The oftener you can turn over the inventory, the better, as long as you keep well supplied according to your needs. If you are using, as an example, $12,000 worth of food a month and have an average inventory of $3,000, this means that you are turning it over four times, which is good. However, if your average inventory is $12,000, then you have only one turnover, which is not good. This too is an easy figure to compute and will quickly tell you whether or not you are carrying too much stock.

Customer Counts

This is another figure not too widely used but a very valuable one to have, as an addition to the dollar sales. Many companies, because of price increases, have shown growth in sales that would indicate that they were doing all right, but if their customer count is dropping, it is a signal that something is wrong, and corrective measures should be taken. Perhaps the price increases were too large, and if the customer count continues to drop, it won't be long before the dollar sales will also show a decrease.

Sales per Server

Here we have another very useful figure that can easily be obtained each day to determine the efficiency of either the servers handling sales at tables or those behind a self-service line. If there are wide variations in the amounts, then either you have some employees who are not producing or there is something wrong with the system and layout being used. Many have not bothered to analyze this figure because they do not pay these people very much money; in the case of table service, most of the pay depends on tips. However, whether we are paying or they are getting tips, it is important to check and see how they are doing. If one server is far below the others in sales, it is a certainty that his tips will not be very high and you will have to replace him sooner or later. A lack of system and good training for servers on a self-service line can mean that you will require more of them and still give bad service.

It is important that we measure the efficiency and productivity of all employees—not only for the sake of the operation, but for their own good. If they are not able to meet the average, perhaps they need some individual help and attention to make them more efficient and better employees.

Average Hourly Wage

This can also be another good bit of information for management. It is another easy figure to compute—the total number of hours, divided into the total dollar payroll. This can quickly tell you if you are in line with other operations, and also let you know when you get out of balance within your own facility.

If you have a higher percentage of skilled employees, who are getting more money per hour, than your average wage will be higher, and you must produce more sales per man-hour to maintain a budget wage-percentage figure. In brief, the higher the average wage you are paying, the more you must produce and the more you should expect from each employee; otherwise, you will be in trouble.

Weekly Purchases

Totals on this should be kept for each week and be checked carefully by management to see that they are in line with the sales, or else you could be building up a huge inventory that is not needed. For the sake of explanation, let's assume that you want to make a 50 percent food cost, and your sales are $10,000 per week. The food purchases each week, then, should be somewhere around the $5,000 figure. If purchases keep running higher than this amount week after week, this is a good indication that something is wrong.

Sales Relationships

Many keep weekly records and percentages on this—for example, the ratio of liquor sales to food sales, or the percentage of the total sales accounted for by wine. Some who want to promote dessert sales even figure this percentage, to see how well they are going. We know that profits on beverages are high, and of course we want to sell as much of them as possible. If we know the relationship each week, it is easy to tell when the servers are not selling as much as they should, and action can be taken to increase these sales.

There are many more figures that can be calculated and used—even down to the amount of butter used as a percentage of sales. Years ago when we had a lot of help, it was easy to keep more detailed records, but now, with the shortage and higher wages, it has become necessary to work with fewer figures, and only the ones we can afford to keep and use. However, too many have dropped more control figures than was wise and seem to be trying to "fly by the seat of their pants," which is not a good idea. We must know what we are doing to some extent and go with the facts and figures; this is not a guessing game.

All the figures and guidelines given above can be kept by the average operation without too much effort. In fact, many places could change accounting systems, save considerable time on reports they are now making that are not really helping the operation, and go to these easier and more valuable figures.

Think of these figures as warning signals—if you have the right ones, each week you can tell at a glance if something is going wrong. Once you have received the warning, immediate action can be taken, so the monthly profit and loss statement will not come as a shock.

SUMMARY

1. *Purposes.* The reason for the necessity of gathering guideline figures is that financial statements are generally placed in management's hands too late for adjustments to be made that can save money. Knowing from day to day, or even hour to hour, how the operation is doing can enable a manager to pinpoint an area or a person that needs quick help, and to take immediate action. Forecasting—anticipating events that will cause business to increase or decline—is invaluable in permitting changes in operation to avoid under- or oversupply of materials and personnel.

2. *Areas.* Many departments of a food service operation are affected by forecasting and guideline figures, because of seasonal changes in business, special events, day-to-day requirements, and price changes. Those areas most in need of this information are purchasing, personnel, food preparation, and menus. Of course, the entire area of budgeting depends on these data; the budget should not be determined by a rigid set of goals, or by industry averages, but rather by the figures relating to the particular circumstances of the individual operation.

3. *Figures Needed.* The most essential of the data that should be collected and used by management are these: (1) sales: weekly and hourly; by item; per man hour; per server; and (of certain items) as a percentage of the total; (2) costs: of food, weekly; of wages, weekly and average hourly;

and of purchases, weekly and as a percentage of sales; (3) inventory turnover; and (4) customer counts.

QUESTIONS FOR REVIEW

In all the following questions, assume that you are the manager of a medium-priced restaurant in your own home town.

1. What sort of seasonal variations or events would you use to forecast changes in the amount of your business?

2. Your operation is equipped with a computerized register system. Which of the guideline figures explained in this chapter could you obtain directly from the tallies rung up on it?

3. What information could you gather from a daily reading of *The Wall Street Journal* that would help you in forecasting? in budgeting?

4. Suppose a trade magazine has reported that the national average for food costs in medium-priced restaurants last month was 32 percent of sales. Your cost was 37 percent. Can you conclude that your operation is in trouble? If so, what steps should you take? If not, what might be the reasons for the difference?

14

Outside Assistance

Objectives

In seeking to improve his business, the owner or manager of a good service operation should not neglect the many outside sources of assistance currently available. When he has studied this chapter, the student should be able to:

1. List many sources of outside help for the industry.
2. Relate the possible costs of such help to the value of its return.
3. Associate types of problems with the sources where assistance in solving them may be obtained.

All of us must continually search for new ideas and better methods, no matter how well we are doing or how long we have been in business. The more assistance we can get in these efforts, the better for the future of any operation, whatever its type of size.

There is a tremendous amount of outside help available to our industry, and most of it is free or costs very little. Many do not realize that this vast area of help is available, and there are those who do not want any help at all, preferring to go it on their own and resenting any suggestions and ideas. Years ago we had to progress by the trial-and-error method, because all this information and knowledge was not available. This learning the hard way might be all right for some, but it is very costly and time-consuming. We must learn to be more efficient, to be open to change and improvement, and to engage in an interchange of ideas from all parts of the industry, if progress is to be made in the future.

This chapter will list quite a few possible sources for outside help and assistance. There are more, but by examining this list, you will soon see that help is available to anyone and can be obtained at very little cost.

Food Service Consultants

There are hundreds of consultants, scattered all over the country, who specialize in the food service industry. They do planning and layouts, select equipment, and can even help with problems connected with the operation itself. Even though there is a fee for their services, in most cases they can save a lot of time and money in the planning by knowing exactly what should be done. The other advantage to using consultants is that they have had years of experience, have seen and worked with all kinds of operations, have learned to take the best ideas from many places, and can put them together quickly to solve your immediate problems.

Just as you would not attempt to plead your own case in a court of law, perform your own surgery, or attempt to make out a very difficult tax form without professional help, you should seek professional help if your facility is in trouble or if you are planning a new one. A bad plan, poor layout, or wrong selection of equipment may or may not cause you to fail, but will almost certainly result in operating losses that will continue for years and years.

Architects and Engineers

In remodelings, changes, and new construction, the services of architects and engineers are a must today, because of the many regulations and codes that must be followed in food service. There was a time when these jobs could be done on almost a do-it-yourself basis, but now it would be advisable to engage good experienced professional help in this field.

All such work must, of course, be approved in advance of building by a number of departments and agencies. There have been too many instances in which people in our business have gone ahead on their own without prior approval, only to find out later that they must make expensive changes before they are able to get operating permits. A competent architect can often save you a lot of money in planning because he knows exactly what should be done and the best way to do it.

Attorney and Tax Specialists

It is essential today to get this professional assistance, because of the many possible legal difficulties that arise. Most businesses either have their own attorney or engage legal help on a continuing basis, not only to handle these various problems, but often, to provide advice before important decisions are made, in order to keep the client from getting into difficulty.

Equally important are the tax specialists, who can advise you of the best method for filling returns and save a lot of grief and headaches in the department. Here again, a fee is involved. You may be reluctant to pay the money, but if the situation calls for good advice, then the payment will be worthwhile in most instances, because litigation can be very costly and damaging to any operation if not handled correctly.

Banks

Modern banks can offer many services to their depositors. In fact, they have expanded these services greatly over the years and are still adding to them. They can be of great assistance in a number of ways. Many employ very knowledgeable people on a full-time basis to help with all kinds of money matters, and most of this advice can be obtained at no cost, or very little.

Insurance Companies

Most people think of insurance as something that you buy to compensate you for disasters after they have happened. But because insurance companies don't like to pay out money, they are happy to send in trained specialists who can survey your operation and give good advice in many areas, so that you can avoid many accidents and other difficulties. As I mentioned in the chapter on safety, they will carefully check your whole facility without charge and point out to you all the places and areas that could cause trouble and accidents. In addition, they can make sure that you are properly covered in all areas; for example, if your fire coverage has not been updated and you have a major fire, it is possible that there would not be enough money to cover the losses and accomplish the rebuilding.

Salesmen

Very often, the representatives of food, equipment, or other supply houses can be most helpful to you in many ways. They can keep you informed on the new products and ideas that could help your own operation. Since they call on and see so many different places, they may be able to give you good ideas on problems that you might be having. We pointed out before that you cannot spend hours each day just chatting with a great number of salesmen, but at the same time, it is good to keep in contact with these people, because they can lend a lot of valuable assistance when needed.

Equipment Dealers

All types of food service need constant contact with equipment dealers who supply the hundreds of items needed each month. It pays to visit their showrooms once in a whole, just to browse around and see what is new that might help you. Or you can call the dealer and explain your problem, and often he can help with the solution.

Equipment Manufacturers

In addition to fabricators that will make up special equipment for you to suit your needs, there are many manufacturers who make a wide range of standard equipment that could be very helpful to your facility. Not only are they trying to develop standard equipment at lower prices for you, but many are now developing complete systems that have been field-tested for greater efficiency. For example, many now sell complete warehandling systems that include everything, including the tables and racks, to give you a very efficient system to handle this most difficult task. Others make complete control systems for food and beverages, and can come in and tailor just the right system to take care of your needs. In other words, they do not just sell equipment today, but have spent a great deal of time, money, and research developing entire tried and proved systems that can be of great help to us.

Many not only sell the equipment but will send in trained people to demonstrate it and assist you in the training of your employees for its best use. Take advantage of as much of this help as you can, because it will be necessary for everyone to know how to use this new equipment and understand the procedures.

Power Companies

Most gas and electric companies maintain separate departments that specialize in commercial food service and are always ready to assist with all kinds of problems you might be having. Some of their services are mobile training and show units for equipment, to demonstrate its proper use and handling; food specialists who can often help you with your food problems; and repair service for your equipment. If your utility bills are too high, they will come in to investigate, and can often point out things you can do to reduce this cost.

By all means, keep in touch with your power company and take advantage of all the extra help and advice they can provide for you.

Health Authorities

Most of us think of the health department as just the people who come in at exactly the wrong time to make an inspection and give us a low score for cleanliness. Actually, they would prefer to work with you to see that you do not have sanitary and food-handling problems, and if you cooperate with them, they can do much to help you in this area. They can look at any plans in advance and advise where you have made mistakes or forgotten some very important item. They are willing to come in at any time and check your premises to give you their ideas on how conditions could be improved. In all these areas, it is much better to work on a preventive basis than on a crash or crisis plan. Try to correct all the little things in advance that could cause a lot of trouble or cost you much more money in the long run.

Chamber of Commerce

Your local chamber of commerce stands ready to supply you with a lot of information that could be valuable to you. It can furnish you with population figures (numbers and density), give figures on business and potential business, enable you to better understand the local market, supply average-earnings figures, define your potential market, and give you a great deal of other information that will help you to merchandise better and to make important decisions.

Local Organizations

There are any number of local civic clubs and groups in your area, and it might pay for you to belong to one or more, as you wish. Becoming involved in the local community can very often be helpful to your business; in addition, it will give you a chance to meet the other business leaders and others in your community who may be of some help to you as problems arise.

Trade Associations

There are many trade associations for the food service industry—local, state, and national. Here again, active participation on your part can be most beneficial. You will meet others in the same field of endeavor, learn what is going on in your industry, get an understanding of legislative problems, have the use of educational and training materials they make available, listen to guest speakers, and attend association shows where you can see new items and ideas and talk with knowledgeable people in the industry.

These associations have much to offer in the way of advice and help, but the amount you derive depends solely on you. If you think you know all there is to know about the business and have a closed mind, or view these associations as merely social, or a means for recognition of your importance, then you will not gain much from the time and effort you put forth.

Books and Pamphlets

There are hundreds and hundreds of good books available covering all phases of our industry, as well as many pamphlets on training, maintenance, sanitation, safety, and so on, that can be of great help to all in the industry. Once again, you can learn the hard way or you can take advantage of the advice and experience of others who have gone through the mill. Much of the material may not apply to your own situation, and you may not agree with all of it, but just a few good ideas from others can sometimes mean a lot of quick help for some of the problems you are having. Learn early in your career not only to recognize your difficulties, but to make every effort to find the solutions as quickly as possible and then make the corrections needed.

Trade Magazines

We now have many food service industry magazines that are available to all. In fact, many will be sent to you free of charge if you will take the trouble to write for them. Some are weekly, some monthly, and some quarterly; even if you have only a little time, just scanning a few regularly can supply much needed and helpful information. For example, one such publication publishes a menu-popularity survey about twice a year, to show what the public tastes are; this alone could help you write your menus and build business. Most have referral cards so that you can easily write for additional information on ideas and products that are of interest to you. Don't just get the publications that apply only to your segment—get as many as possible, because you might see something in a fast-food magazine that would help you if you are in the in-plant feeding business.

Exchange of Ideas

Visit all the other operations you can. Meet the owners and operators, and learn to discuss and exchange ideas. There are no secrets in the business now, and this interchange can be most helpful to all parties. This is a two-way street; when other operators come to visit your operation, be sure that they are shown everything they would like to see. In the process of giving, you will also receive.

Outside Services

There are many companies now supplying all kinds of services to our industry, and you should investigate this area as much as possible. They can take much of the labor problem off your back and provide valuable assistance in the preventive field, in such areas as window cleaning, large cleaning jobs, lawn maintenance, bug and pest control, rug cleaning, equipment maintenance, and so on. Good companies usually have well-trained people who are specialists in their field, and even though the price might seem high, you must realize that if you attempt to do all this yourself, the end cost could be even higher. Then, too, you want to concentrate on the business of serving food, not washing windows, doing mechanical work, trying to kill bugs, or any of the other difficult jobs that your own crew is not trained to do.

General Contractors

When there are large repair jobs of remodelings to be done, they should be turned over to a general contractor. This work usually involves a number of different trades, and the hiring, coordinating, and supervision can be rather time-consuming. Many think they can save money by being their own general contractors and supervising the job, but once again, we should stick to the business of serving food and turn as much of this other kind of work over to people who know what they are doing.

In most cases, a general contractor will give you a total price for the job, and it is easy to tell very soon whether or not this will fit into your program or budget for the job. If you attempt to engage all the subcontractors and supervise the job yourself, you have no way of telling what the total will be at the end.

Police and Fire Departments

You should cooperate with the police department in every way possible; not only can they be of great assistance in emergencies—robberies, break-ins, or other matters that need investigation—but they can supply a protection service for your facility when you are closed. They too have trained people who can come in, inspect your premises carefully, and advise if you have the proper safeguards against burglaries and other crimes. For instance, they can tell you if your safe is in the right place and of the right kind, what lights to keep on at night, and whether you have the right type of door locks.

The fire department, in addition to being on instant call for fires you cannot handle, can also give you much the same advisory service free—tell you of any fire hazards you might have and where fires are most apt to start, advise the best kind of extinguishers for you and what will be best for grease and electric fires. They are very interested in keeping you from having fires that will be costly to you and will hurt your business.

Too often, we think of departments like this as performing their services only when there is a dire emergency, but they also devote a great deal of time and work to prevention of these happenings. Use the services they present, and by all means follow their instructions as closely as possible.

Advertising Agencies

Back in the chapter on merchandising, it was mentioned that you might want to spend some money for advertising and promotion, and this is a good idea. When you are ready and the time is ripe, go to a good advertising agency and discuss the entire program. Let them tell you how to get the most for every dollar you are going to spend, because they have the experience and know-how, particularly in your area, and probably can suggest the way to attract the most business for the money. Today, with all the media available—radio, television, newspapers, billboards, publications—it is difficult for the inexperienced to tell which would be best or how much money to spend. Then, too, this job must be done right to produce the best results; if the effort is weak, the results will be the same. It may not cost as much money to put up a cheap road sign saying, "Eat at Joe's Place 2 miles down the road," but you also won't get much in the way of results from the money spent.

Food Processors

Many of these people are now in a position to help you with your food problems. There are many hundreds of large food-processing companies that are continually working on new foods and systems that eventually could assist your own facility. They are spending millions of dollars on testing— bringing out products that will save you money, time, and effort—so it would be wise to at least see what they have and can do for you.

Here again, there are those in our business who still say they know more about this, and can do it better and cheaper than these huge companies can, but it would be worth your time to prove this to yourself. Don't take for granted what either side says; actually spend some time and see for yourself.

Special Maintenance

You might be involved in an operation that has some special problems in certain areas. If, for instance, you have your own sewage-disposal plant, or your own water systems, these are conditions that will need special care and attention. In many cases, these services will be very important to your business, and interruptions could cost money and business. When you run into these conditions, then by all means arrange for special maintenance service on a regular basis, to protect yourself.

Large-Quantity Recipes

Good recipes are available from many sources. Most are printed on cards that are easy to file and use, and have portion-control and yield figures that will help you in your production. Again, you can set up your own recipes by trial and error and spend a great deal of time developing a file, but instead of this long and expensive route, at least try some of the recipes that have already been developed, tried, and tested. Often, if you are not completely satisfied, you can make a slight adjustment to one of them and get the end result much sooner.

This list of outside-assistance sources should convince you that you can get all the help you need, and, in many cases, at very little cost or effort. The important thing is that you take advantage of this—learn to profit by what others have gone through and the mistakes they have made. What will help most is that you seek help, learn to accept advice from others who have had the experience, and then follow the suggestions. Perhaps you might want to make slight changes in some things, or add a little of your own imagination and creative ability. This is fine and there is nothing wrong with the idea, but it is wrong to think that you can do everything better and cheaper than others.

In the Appendix that follows the next chapter, you will find a list of professional food service consultants, constituting the membership of two prestigious trade societies—the International Society of Food Service Consultants and the Food Facilities Consultants Society—as well as a list of trade publications and books.

SUMMARY

1. *Outside Aid.* Assistance in solving many problems in the food service industry is available today, from sources outside the industry as well as from support segments. Since the problems are many, management should take advantage of this assistance as much as possible.

2. *Sources.* Sources of assistance are support indus-

tries, such as food service consultants, equipment manufacturers and dealers, food processors, salesmen, and the many sources of large-quantity recipes; the professions, such as architects, engineers, attorneys, and tax specialists; institutions, such as banks, insurance companies, and power companies; service companies, such as maintenance, contractors, and advertising agencies; government, such as health authorities and police and fire departments; organizations, such as chambers of commerce, trade associations, and local organizations; print, such as books, pamphlets, and trade magazines; and also the exchange of ideas with other members of the industry.

3. *Cost and Availability.* The sources listed here are available to all who need their help. Some of them charge for their services and some do not, but in most cases, if the source is qualified, the results will more than repay any fee required.

QUESTIONS FOR REVIEW

1. If you were planning to build a new food service facility in an area that was relatively unfamiliar to you, which of the sources listed in this chapter would you go to for assistance? (Save your answer to this question for reference in the next chapter.)

2. In reference to question 1, what information and/or service would you request from each?

3. After the place was built but before it opened, which sources would you make use of?

15

Planning and Equipment

Objectives

Starting a new food service facility and remodeling an existing one—the elements of food service planning—are the topics covered in this chapter. After completing it, the student should be able to:

1. Name circumstances under which remodeling may be needed.
2. List the data that planners need for remodeling or for building a new facility.
3. Relate much of the information given in previous chapters to the requirements of planning.

Proper planning, layout, and equipment play a very important role in the successful operation of any food service operation today. Years ago, we could offset poor planning by adding enough employees to accomplish the job to be done, but now we must do even more business with fewer people who are not as skilled and well trained. However, by doing a lot of research and study on factors like work and product flow, we have been able to increase the productivity of the employees we do have. The waste of effort caused by unnecessary steps and motion can be eliminated by good layout and planning, and, of course, the much better equipment we have now helps to replace the skill that we can no longer find.

There is still a long way to go in the battle to increase productivity in the food service industry, but with the cooperation of professional planners and equipment manufacturers, progress is being made.

NEW AND REMODELED FACILITIES

There are two major parts to food service planning—designing the new facilities, and remodeling the existing operations so that they can be more efficient. With the hundreds of thousands of existing facilities, the job of remodeling will be the most important in the future. We know that it is not difficult to design new operations correctly, but it is often hard to change the facilities already in operation so that they will be better and give improved results. In this introductory text, it will not be possible to get into all the fine points and details of making layouts and plans and selecting equipment, but we can

253

stress some of the major considerations and give some examples of new equipment that is available.

Because the right plan is so essential, the most important consideration is that professional help be engaged as soon as possible, whether it be a new operation or a remodeling. Many make the mistake of attempting to do this work themselves or hiring an unqualified person at what looks like a saving. The fact that well-qualified help is available is clearly shown by the lists of food service planners given in the Appendix, people who are located in all parts of this country and of the world. These consultants have had wide experience in designing all kinds of operations; their help can not only save money in the investment cost, but produce facilities that will operate at lower costs over the years.

REMODELING

Reasons for Remodeling

A decision to remodel could be prompted by one or more of several reasons.

Greater Demand. Expansion may be needed because the business has increased or the demand is greater. Schools are called upon to feed more students, hospitals must add more beds, correctional institutions must care for more inmates. Whatever the circumstance, the existing facility for serving food must either be enlarged or changed so that it can handle more people.

Refurbishing. Remodeling is often needed when the facility has become old and worn and needs to be given a new look or have badly worn equipment replaced with new. Nothing lasts forever, not even food service equipment, so the time comes for replacements.

Competition. We are constantly faced with the job of meeting competition, which is becoming more acute each day. Much of our competition comes from new operations, either chain or individually operated; these come in with totally new plants and facilities that are not only more attractive to the guests, but more efficient to operate than the place that is ten or fifteen years old. It is impossible to win the Kentucky Derby with an old plow horse, and it may be equally hard for an old, worn-out facility to compete with a new and highly productive competitor.

Efficiency. Another reason for changing is simply the fact that the old facility is no longer efficient enough to match today's conditions. A manager can do just so much to reduce operating costs like payroll with a poor layout; the time invariably comes when other actions must be taken. Because many of the older facilities were designed when help was plentiful and cheap, the kitchens and other vital areas were planned to need many more employees than we now have and can afford to use.

Quicker Service. The need to speed service in all kinds of operations can also demand remodeling and changes in many areas. If the kitchen is old and improperly manned, the servers will have difficulty getting their orders; if the warehandling is inadequate and located in a bad spot, this will cause trouble with the service; if the dining areas are poorly located, causing excessive walking, we can expect even more delays. Most of these deficiencies can be corrected in a well-planned remodeling.

Upgrading. Finally many older operations need "upgrading"—improving the appearance and changing methods of service so that new foods can be served and check averages increased.

Whatever the reason for change and improvement, any remodeling must be carefully planned so that the operation really benefits from the work and effort and, most important, so that increased sales and profits will return the investment in as short a time as possible.

Information Needed

Even though the owners and principals should not themselves attempt to make the plans and layouts and select the new equipment, they can assist in the project by gathering all the information possible before the planning actually starts, so that when the consultant and other planners start their work, they will have vital and reliable facts and figures to work with. One cannot correct errors and make improvements without knowing what exists and what the owner wishes to accomplish. The more data collected on the existing facility in advance, the easier it will be for the consultant to make a new plan that will produce the results needed. Following are the items of information that will be needed before a line can be drawn on paper.

Menus. Copies of all the current menus should be gathered—breakfast, luncheon, dinner, late supper, children's, bar, wine lists, banquet, take-out, and so on. These will inform the planners of what items are to be served and when.

Prices. Price ranges are important because they determine how many people must be served in a given time to produce the needed income.

Operating Time. It is very important in planning to know when the operation will be open. In the case of school lunches, for instance, it is known that only luncheon will be served, and on only about 180 days of the year, so that less equipment will be needed than in an operation that is open for 18 hours a day, every day of the year, serving all meals plus other functions such as parties and banquets.

Number of Employees. Not only should the total number be noted, but the list should be broken down into the number in each department—food preparation, control, food service, food serving, and so forth. This will not only help in determining what employee facilities are needed, but will also give a good idea of the areas and equipment needed for all the new departments.

Seating. The exact number of seats must be known, and they should be listed as to the size of the tables—twos, fours, sixes, and so on. It is possible in many cases to rearrange the seating and change to table sizes that give a higher turnover with the same total number of seats.

Parking. Unless it is a pure "walk-up" operation, the number of parking spaces for the customers must be known. It is foolish to increase the seating if enough additional parking spaces cannot be added to take care of this increased business.

Customer Counts. Whether it is a commercial facility or an institutional one, definite figures must be provided on the number to be fed, and these figures must be broken down into the various serving times.

Market. All this means is that you must describe the type of people you are feeding—by age, occupation, income level, and so on—so that the new operation will still fit the customer. On the other hand, if you wish to change your market and perhaps shoot for a different class, this fact should be noted.

Item Tallies. In addition to the menus and the number of people served, it is important to know exactly what items are being served and how many. It is not enough to say, "We serve a lot of fried food"—the planners have to know what the fried foods are and the amounts of each that are sold. Then they can provide exactly the kinds and capacities of fryers needed.

All Services. In addition to the regular meals served, the facility may offer take-out, parties, catering, room service, bar, lounges, and other types of food service. All of these must be known in advance so that proper areas and equipment can be provided to handle these functions well.

Productivity Figures. Many operations do not have these. In simple terms, these figures tell how many dollars of sales you do in a given time—a week, day, or year—per man-hour or full-time employee. In the case of institutions, it would be meals served in place of dollars. If this information is known in advance of the planning, it is easy to tell just how efficient the old facility is, indicating the amount of change needed to bring the efficiency up to the average, or better than average.

Food Preparation. Describe in detail not only what food items are prepared on the premises, but the degree of preparation. Are all the foods prepared from scratch, or are convenience foods used to lessen this burden? Is there need for a complete bake shop, or butcher shop, or can most of this work be eliminated? By changing food-preparation methods, it is possible to effect savings in space, equipment, and number of employees, and reduce the operating costs in the newly remodeled facility.

Public Rest Rooms. These are very often neglected in planning. While codes will indicate the absolute minimum number of fixtures needed for various sizes of operations, we should go further to make these rest rooms as attractive and comfortable as possible. In addition, they should be located in a convenient spot where they can be found without creating cross traffic through congested areas. All the materials used (floors, walls, etc.) should be easy to clean and maintain. (You can now install fixtures and partitions that are off the floor to make cleaning a simpler task.) A dirty rest room with towels all over the floor, fixtures that do not work, or dirty walls and floors can sometimes spoil a guest's entire visit to a restaurant.

Employee Facilities. These are often neglected in planning because of space or money shortages. Most health codes now require separate rest rooms for employees, but even if they don't, this is an excellent idea for all restaurants, for kitchen personnel are often not too presentable and should therefore be kept apart from public facilities. In addition to employees having their own rest rooms, it is also advisable to provide them with dressing areas and lockers. Most of the food service employees wear uniforms and must change clothing. In addition, they need lockers where their personal items can be safely stored while they are on duty. Employees should also be provided with a separate area for eating their meals, smoking, and taking much needed breaks. Not having these simple features can often cause annoyances that will result in resignations and increased labor turnover.

Management must have an office: a place to work and keep records, interview salesmen, talk with employees, and so on. This office should be air conditioned and as quiet as possible; it can be located in an area where it is still possible to watch the important parts of the operation at all times.

Traffic and Product Flow. One of the most important considerations in all planning is to first establish all flow patterns and then detail the equipment and fixtures. Make sure that customer parking is as close to the entrance as possible, rest rooms and public waiting areas are on a direct line from entrance to seating areas, waitress service aisles are located with proper in and out doors to avoid cross traffic and minimize confusion in dining areas, the warewashing is centrally located so that soiled ware can be easily brought in and clean ware can be quickly taken back to points of use such as service stands and kitchens. Your product and material flow should be planned on a straight line as much as possible, making for a natural flow through the operation. This in itself will eliminate much of the cross traffic. Materials should come in, go to bulk storage, to point of use storage, to preparation, to service, and then directly to the customer. Studying your traffic and product flow very carefully in planning stages can save you a lot in wasted motion, steps, and confusion. Remember that food service employees spend 25 percent of their time walking. When you are walking you are not producing, and most of this excess motion is caused because someone failed to study the traffic and product flow carefully when making the plans and layouts.

Profit and Loss Statements. The owner and the planners should go over these figures carefully to note exactly where the troubles are and what needs improving. If the replacement cost for china and glassware is too high, for example, the consultant will know that some time must be spent in designing a better warehandling system.

Zoning and Regulations. The owner should find out from the government agencies all the regulations that will apply to the change. Getting this information in advance can save a lot of time and effort in making plans that will not be approved. Many regulations are not enforced for existing facilities; if you start making major changes and drawing plans, enforcement of the regulations may be renewed.

Area Growth. Figures on this can be obtained from local organizations like the chamber of commerce. If the population is expected to double in size within a few years, perhaps even more expansion is indicated; if the population or market might decrease, then the plans should be made so that you can operate with less business and still make a profit.

Existing Problems. Actually write down all the problems with the facility as it is. This involves meeting with your employees to find out where they are having trouble. If you are having a problem getting the food to the servers, for instance, put this on the list so that the consultant will know and can design to eliminate this problem.

Objectives. By all means, list all the things you want in the new operation. Perhaps it will not be possible to achieve all your goals, but make the list as complete as possible. If you don't do this in advance, it will mean many unnecessary changes in plans and drawings that will not only delay the project but run up the cost.

In summary, for remodeling projects, we must provide in advance all the statistics available on the existing operation. If any of those mentioned above are not available, then they should be gathered, even if only for a short period. It is important also to detail all the objectives desired, so that the planning can be arranged to fulfill them as nearly as possible. The central idea is that the time, money, and effort spent should produce some real advantages that will justify them and compensate for them in a reasonable length of time.

NEW PROJECTS

In many respects, it is easier to plan new projects than to remodel, because we are free to design the facility as it should be. Many times in remodelings, compromises are necessary when it is impossible to change the existing plans and buildings to provide what is really needed, because the cost would be too great to justify the change. But if the new project is designed in the right order, we should come up with a plan that will work well and do the job required.

Here again, it is important that we follow a logical sequence, to avoid many changes to the design and plans along the way. For example, it is best to engage the consultant for the food service first, let him make the preliminary layouts and space allocations that will be needed to accomplish the goals, and then hire the architect. This not only will save the owners time and money but will save the architect a lot of time in trying to guess what is needed or required. If the consultant for the food service is forced to work with completed plans that are not right or adequate, he will find it difficult to come up with the right plan for the new project.

We will need the same information set forth under remodeling when we get into new planning, but with the difference that we must project or estimate these facts and figures. However, we can use the same list (menus, number of employees, market, and so on) and then project what can be expected. There are methods by which we can do this job fairly accurately; perhaps we will not be right on all counts, but at least the end result will be better than if we engage in "blind" planning, as is so often done. For example, it is entirely possible to make up a menu in advance, even indicating the price levels desired. This can give the planners some valuable information on which to base their designs and selection of equipment. Many places have been designed without a menu in advance, but it is easy to see that such a practice makes the layout difficult to determine—it would be like designing a factory without knowing the product to be manufactured.

Good planning is a result of knowing and answering the famous five W's—*who, what, when, where,* and *why.* It is not difficult to come up with good plans and layouts that will produce results, but some careful preplanning is needed.

SELECTION OF EQUIPMENT

In either a remodeling or a new venture, once the preliminary building plans have been determined, the time comes to select the equipment needed. Professional help is advised here, because in view of the hundreds of companies making equipment, with an equal number of catalogs listing and showing many different models, sizes, and capacities, it is easy to see that this is no job for an amateur. Nowadays, it involves much more than just picking out a few ranges or refrigerators, because today's equipment can do many things for any operation, new or old.

Right Amount and Size

If the person selecting the equipment is not fully qualified, the operation can end up with too much equipment or not enough to do the job. Overequipping will result not only in excess investment cost in the equipment, but in added building space, which is very costly.

Ease of Cleaning

Cleaning is both a time-consuming job and quite an expense. However, all equipment today (except items rigidly connected to water, steam, and drains) can be purchased on wheels and casters, so that is is easily cleaned and can be moved from department to department for multiple use.

Standard Models

Almost all the equipment needed in modern food service installations can be purchased in standard form, direct from catalogs, at lower prices than would be paid for custom-designed and fabricated items.

Replacement of Skills and Experience

Much of the equipment today is automated (or semi-automated), with controls, timers and other devices built in to replace the skilled food-preparation and service cooks we have lost. In short, we are able to produce higher-quality foods more consistently.

Examples of Equipment

It would be impossible to illustrate and describe all the equipment available, but we can look into a few typical pieces to show what is available and the trend in equipment design and manufacturing. Some of those to be shown are not major pieces, but the use of even these smaller items can help production and increase efficiency.

Even this limited selection of illustrations indicates the huge variety of equipment available to help the food service industry. The trick is the selection of the right pieces in the right quantity and sizes to do your job well. Professional help in this job is highly recommended.

FIGURE 15-1

Vertical Cutter/Mixer

Here is an interesting piece of equipment that is finding much acceptance in preparation areas because it is versatile—it can be used for all kinds of cutting work, and serves as a mixer as well. In short, this could replace two expensive machines in a preparation kitchen.

FIGURE 15-2

Infrared Oven

Another versatile piece of equipment, used for heating, roasting, and browning, and very adaptable for reconstituting the many frozen foods now available.

FIGURE 15-3

Commercial Sectionizer

A small, hand-operated piece of equipment that can serve many purposes and save a lot of expensive labor with very little investment.

FIGURE 15-4

Grapefruit Sectionizer

Another interesting small, hand-operated piece of equipment, an example of the devices made now that can do away with many of the old, slow, hand methods of doing things.

FIGURE 15-5

Lettuce Cutter/Slicer

Here again, we have a simple machine of low cost that can cut those production costs and speed service.

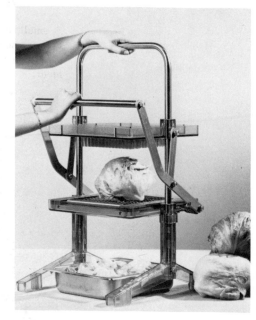

FIGURE 15-6

Roll-In Convection Oven

Convection ovens have gained in popularity and use over the years because they bake and roast faster at lower temperatures, producing better products with less fuel cost. Now they are being made with new features that permit you, for example, to roll in entire racks of products and remove them quickly.

*Stainless Steel with
Iron Grill Surface*

All Stainless Steel

FIGURE 15-7

Tilting Fry Pan

A very versatile piece of equipment, first introduced from abroad, that can do many different jobs — from cooking soups and stews to frying chicken, steaks, or chops, and even grilling cheese sandwiches in quantity.

FIGURE 15-8

Convection Steamer

Food steamers have been on the market for many years, but now they are being designed with new features. An example is this convection steamer, which agitates the steam around the product. This steamer also permits the door to be safely opened at any time during the cooking, for adding or removing items without interrupting the cooking sequence or timing.

FIGURE 15-9

The Cafeteria in the Round

An interesting recent development that several companies are producing to change the old routine of self-service. Instead of the customer's moving from food to food, he stands in one place and the foods come around for his selection.

FIGURE 15-10

Computerized Fryer

This is an example of replacing employee skill. This fryer adjusts to the kinds and quantities of foods placed in it and ensures that they are cooked just right every time.

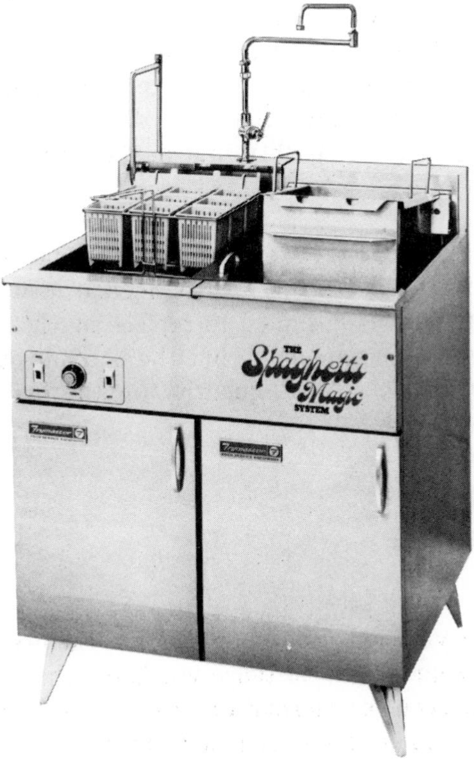

FIGURE 15-11

Spaghetti System

A highly specialized piece of equipment, but one that solves a difficult problem we have had for years—how to cook and serve spaghetti well in quantity. This machine provides for cooking the initial large amount, washing it, storing it cold water, and then heating measured servings as needed.

SUMMARY

1. *Planning.* Food service planning has two major classifications: designing new facilities and remodeling existing ones. Remodeling is more difficult, since it requires correcting errors and working within the limitations of existing operations. The necessity for remodeling may be caused by an increase in demand, the need to update or upgrade, the impact of competition, or current lack of efficiency and speed in service.

2. *Information That Planners Need.* Before remodeling starts, management must furnish to the planners the following information: current menus with prices and tallies of items sold, number and jobs of employees, operating hours, numbers of seats and parking spaces, type and counts of customers, additional services provided, figures on productivity and profit and loss, on-premises food preparation, public and employee restrooms, traffic flow diagrams, government regulations that apply, expected area growth, current problem areas, and objectives for the future. The same data are required for the planning of a new facility, but in the form of estimates and forecasts.

3. *Equipment.* Because of the great number of makes and models of equipment, professional help is needed in its selection. Today's equipment is designed to replace much of the skill no longer available in personnel; but the equipment must be of the proper kind, size, and quantity for the best results.

QUESTIONS FOR REVIEW

1. Refer back to your answer to question 1 in the preceding chapter. Of the sources of assistance you listed there, from which would you receive information that you would have to furnish to the planners for your new facility?

2. If you, as manager of an existing operation, had been collecting all the guideline figures listed in Chapter 13, would you have all the operating statistics needed for a remodeling? If not, which would be missing?

3. For class discussion: Of the pieces of equipment illustrated in this chapter, which do you consider the most necessary for a medium-priced, table-service facility that does a lot of business?

Appendix

This section is added to aid both instructors and students. The purpose is not only to show the huge size and organization of the industry, but to illustrate the organizations and sources of valuable information that are available. In all these areas, we find a vast amount of material, resulting from years of experience and study, that will help not only the student just entering the field, but also those actively engaged in all segments of the industry.

A. FOOD SERVICE CONSULTANTS

Here are lists of two prominent societies: the ISFSC (International Society of Food Service Consultants) and the FFCS (Food Facilities Consultants Society). The text mentions the importance of seeking professional help; these people and their organizations are readily available in all parts of the United States and most parts of the world. The addresses of their main offices are listed later in the appendix under "Associations of the Industry."

International Society of Food Service Consultants

A nonprofit organization which provides a professional society for consultants in design, equipment, engineering, and management to the food service industry and furthers research, development and education in the food service field.

Objectives and Code of Ethics

The Society has the purpose of providing professional association among persons meeting the Society's requirements for membership. Professionalization will be fostered through appropriate standards of practice, education, research, the dissemination of knowledge and a high sense of responsibility towards the member's client and the general public.

These objectives will be furthered by:

the compilation and addition to knowledge of the food service field and especially of food service facilities;

the establishment of standards of professional practice among the members;

broadening of the understanding of the problems involved in food service planning;

the encouragement of participation by members in their community and world affairs;

the encouragement of research and the development of improved approaches to food service planning;

the encouragement of teaching of the principles and practices of planning for food service facilities.

Members pledge themselves to work toward:

the establishment of uniform and published fees for their services;

the avoidance of misrepresentation and maintenance of a high standard of honesty in all dealings with clients;

the adjustment of claims and the settlement of disputes on the basis of facts and fairness;

cooperation among members of the Association for the betterment of food service industry;

the free exchange of plans and information concerning the food service industry;

the recognition that at times the members will have to forego personal gain to uphold their honor and serve the general good of the client and the public;

the forebearance from self advertising in any way except that which is dignified and in accordance with a professional society;

the protection of the good name of the Society;

the avoidance of lending professional support knowingly to a device or enterprise that is fraudulent or of no benefit to mankind;

the forbearance of the use of plans prepared by another without acknowledging the source of those plans;

the forbearance from supplanting a fellow consultant after definite steps have been taken toward the other's employment;

the recognition that character is the hallmark of a food service consultant;

the objective that a client or buyer be given the very best possible for the price charged.

Principal Officers

EXECUTIVE SECRETARY
Earl D. Tripplett
Bloomfield Hills, Michigan 48103

EDITOR/PUBLISHER: *THE CONSULTANT*
Asa K. Gaylord

Membership Roster, U.S.A.

ALABAMA
John D. Fellers

ALASKA
Lino Agosti

AMERICAN SAMOA
Henry J. Schaink

ARIZONA
William Bales
Ole Klendshoj

ARKANSAS
Thomas R. Smith

CALIFORNIA
James L. Brown
Paul S. Damazo
Ralph Deffenbaugh
Aubrey Devine, Jr.
William S. Edsall, Jr.
Volker O. Elsasser
Richard Flambert
Joseph W. Laschober
Bert Marshall, Jr.
Jane Ellery Neibert
Wid O. Neibert
Theodore Paulos
Hugh T. Smart
Morris Spievak
William R. West

COLORADO
Harold W. Sheridan

CONNECTICUT
Murray A. Perl
Robert J. Sevieri
Arthur L. Walter

DISTRICT OF COLUMBIA
Malcolm B. McLean

FLORIDA
Ronald C. Appel
Harry Friedman
Hugo Garin
Steven T. Lowell
Donald Vinton
George E. Whitmill
Robert E. Wolf
George G. Zipfel

GEORGIA
James M. Brady
Ezra F. (Ez) Ferris

ILLINOIS
Sig Chakow
Ben J. Freed
Jack McCabe
Casimir C. Mroz
Otto Schlecker

INDIANA
Arthur C. Avery
Arlene M. Wilson

KANSAS
Frederick P. Schoenfeld
Willie C. Taylor

MARYLAND
Gerald Antonuccio
John C. Cini
Anne Claire Donovan
William A. Dorko
Craig C. MacCullough
Rob R. McLallen

Thomas N. Pappas
Henry A. Siegel
C. Ray Sims
Theodore E. White
Lyle E. Wright

MASSACHUSETTS
Morton R. Godine
C. Graham Hurlburt, Jr.
Donald E. Lundberg
Wesley A. McSorley, Jr.
Robert S. Osborne
John W. Stokes
Charles A. Wood

MICHIGAN
Ahmet Dervishi
Carlos Garcia
Paul Hysen
Morton Kaplan
Martin Kohlligian

MINNESOTA
Jan Van Hemert

MISSOURI
William S. Ford
Russell G. Lenz
H. H. Pope
W. Milt Santee
Richard S. Spener
Joseph Vasquez

NEW HAMPSHIRE
Hyman E. Novak

NEW JERSEY
Vincent N. Antonell
Bruce B. Blickman
Murray J. Grohsman
Claude L. Hatecke
Prof. David Hertzson

NEW YORK
John Andrews
Anagnostaras
Philip C. Antico
Bruce H. Axler
John E. Barron
Moshe Chovev
Walter F. Clifford
Dr. Leroi Folsom
Lester L. Forman
Martin Friedman
Frank N. Giampietro
Harry Greitzer
William J. Hrabrick
Robert H. Kaiser
Charles Klain
George J. Kraft
Joseph X. McGinn, Jr.
Benjamin Perlstein
Bruce L. Robertson
Roslyn Willett

NORTH CAROLINA
William M. Rocamora

OHIO
John C. Cini
John A. Ruff
Arthur Stern
Frank L. Swain

OKLAHOMA
Charles B. Jeremiah
Ronald A. Miller

OREGON
Asa K. Gaylord
Edson C. Gaylord

PENNSYLVANIA
Frank O. Carpenter
Charles W. Letier
Richard P. Troyer
Gay H. Welborn

PUERTO RICO
O. Ernest Bangs
Vincente Berdeguer

SOUTH CAROLINA
Donald E. Hoshaw

TENNESSEE
Joe T. Brooks
Theril T. Bush
Carl F. Lilie
James K. Scruggs

TEXAS
Norman Ackerman
Alan L. Berger
Joseph H. Berger
George E. Bond
Ray Randuk
H. G. Rice
A. E. Worley

VIRGINIA
Jordan Gallos
George K. Hawkins

WASHINGTON
Robert E. Cleveland
William W. Manahan
C. Russel Nickel
Robert W. Whitney

Membership Roster, Foreign Countries

CANADA
Gertrude Bernard
Mairi Cochran
William Goodbrand
Larry W. Hart
Hugh Pauwels
Joseph Robinson
Harold A. Rosenberg
John T. Shannon
Milton Shier
Sydney M. Sobel
Rene M. Vandervelde
Charles B. Woods

CHILE
Esteban H. Kemeny

ENGLAND
Hugo Garin

FRANCE
John Andrews
Anagnostaras
Hugo Garin
Pierre Thevenin

GERMANY
Dr. Dietrich Schneider

GREECE
John Andrews
Anagnostaras
Simeon Patrikas

INDIA
   Lalit Nirula
   Narendra Verma

ISRAEL
   Leon A. Sherman

NORWAY
   Karl Einar Gleditsch

PHILIPPINES
   Imelda S. Silayan

SPAIN
   Rafael Alvarez

SWEDEN
   Stig Westberg

SWITZERLAND
   Bruno M. Brivio
   Justus Dahinden
   Edward F. Freytag
   Raoul Emil Illig
   Ueli Prager
   Enrico R. Principi
   Margrit Ursprung

VENEZUELA
   Bela De Holt

Food Facilities Consultants Society

Planning and operation of food service facilities has become more complex and diverse in recent years. The invention of new equipment, the increasing use of convenience and prefabricated foods, and the need for work simplification techniques to combat rising costs has made a professional approach to food facilities planning an absolute necessity.

Members of the Food Facilities Consultants Society are qualified, professional food facility designers, planners, and consultants. In addition to meeting specified eligibility requirements, no member may "be engaged in the manufacture, sale, or promotion of sales of food service equipment or supplies."

Code of Ethics

To define the standards of conduct for the practice of its profession, the Food Facilities Consultants Society, a national nonprofit professional society, has adopted the following *Code of Ethics* for its members' guidance and discipline:

A. PREAMBLE

The performance of professional service calls for men of undoubted integrity, experience; business responsibility, and judgment. A Consultant's honesty of purpose and loyalty to his client must be above suspicion; he acts as professional advisor to his client, and his advice must be unprejudiced. He has moral responsibilities to his professional associates and employees. His acts affect the public health and safety. These duties and responsibilities require that his motives, conduct, and ability are such as to command respect and confidence.

The services of the Food Facilities Consultant include research, planning, technical guidance and advice to the client, and cooperative effort with other building planning professions. Their purpose is to guard the client's interests against errors of judgment and to participate in the planning and construction of public food service facilities which will promote the public health and safety, be efficient and economical to operate and maintain, and be attractive and distinctive.

B. PROFESSIONAL EMPLOYMENT

1. He solicits work only through regularly employed or associated professionals.
2. He offers his services on the basis of ability, facilities for rendering service, and availability.
3. He will withhold any offer to render professional services after definite steps have been taken by a client to engage another consultant.
4. He, knowing that another consultant has been engaged for a project, will undertake a commission for said project only after he has determined that the other consultant's services have been terminated, and he has notified the other consultant in writing of his intent to serve the client.
5. He shall not work at the same time with competing clients except under specific arrangements agreeable to each client.
6. He shall not obtain competitive advantage by means of "donations" or by dividing fees with nonprofessionals.

C. PROFESSIONAL RELATIONS

1. He shall not injure the professional reputation, prospects, or the practice of another consultant.
2. He shall safeguard confidential information and data whether supplied by a client or prepared by himself.
3. He shall promote education, research, and instruction of younger professionals and the public concerning the profession.

D. PROFESSIONAL SERVICE

1. He makes recommendations based upon knowledge of the client's needs and financial limitations, and provides honest and full cooperation with his client and client's representatives.
2. His services shall conform to all applicable laws and regulations of the State and municipality within which he performs professional services.

E. PAYMENT

1. He shall be paid solely by his client by fee, salary, or royalty. He accepts no remuneration, monetary or otherwise, from suppliers or others who deal with his client. His charges are based upon the work involved in the project. He does not work on a speculative basis and must receive appropriate and tangible compensation for all his work.
2. He may accept fees and royalties on government-recognized products of the brain, on which he holds patent or copyright. In the case of a project for a client, where said patented products would be used, the client shall be fully advised by the consultant.

F. BUSINESS PROMOTION

1. He refrains from advertising or self-laudatory statements which reflect on the dignity and integrity of his profession.
2. He issues no publicity with regard to his work without full clearance from his client.

Membership Roster, Geographical Locations

ARIZONA
Donald E. Dedrick

ARKANSAS
Max G. Futch

CALIFORNIA
Anthony A. Clevenger
Paul Fairbrook
Carl B. Hansen
Michael S. Hayden
Richard Kramer
Fred Schmid
Edward S. Sovich
Hank Walraven

COLORADO
Jeff B. Katz
Duane W. Newlin

CONNECTICUT
Jerry O'Rourk

DISTRICT OF
    COLUMBIA
Vincent J. Kelly
C. Ray Sims

FLORIDA
John E. Markham

GEORGIA
Joseph Camacho, Jr.

ILLINOIS
Robert C. Behrens
James A. Belter
Marian Dobrowolski
James E. Kibbee
Eldor A. Kluge

Jack McCabe
James R. Parker
Charles C. Post
Richard M. Scanlan
Robert F. Schmid
Clifford J. Stock

INDIANA
Clarence E. Porter
Sherman Robinson

IOWA
R. Eric Anderson
Chester A. Scott

LOUISIANNA
Max G. Futch

MARYLAND
John C. Cini
William V. Eaton
Gary W. Hughart
Eugene A. Jacobs
Craig C. MacCullough
Michael Mason
James H. Peterson, Jr.
Harry Schildkraut
Francis W. White

MASSACHUSETTS
Samuel Crabtree
Ronald P. Hirtle
Nicholas Kirikos
Robert M. Lindsey
Robert P. McGrath
Anthony T. Michaels

MICHIGAN
E. F. Whitney

MINNESOTA
    Robert D. Rippe
    Jan Van Hemert
    Herbert S. Wiles

MISSOURI
    James H. Dixon
    Dennis G. Glore

NEBRASKA
    Robert E. Owens

NEW JERSEY
    Thomas H. Banks
    Paul P. Busko
    Thomas R. Corby
    Daniel H. Hrubes
    Ferdinand P. Lidonnici
    R. Joseph Raymond, Jr.
    Robert V. Reinhardt

NEW YORK
    Samuel S. Arlen
    Ira B. Beer
    Frank S. Carey
    Charles King Emma
    Richard E. Fletcher
    Stanley D. Gatland
    Frank N. Giampietro
    Roland E. Greaves
    Alfred T. Jacobsen
    Robert E. Reinhold
    Salvatore N. Romano
    Harry T. Skolodz
    Albert J. Zaralban

NORTH CAROLINA
    Joseph Camacho, Jr.

OHIO
    Jeffrey Derrow

Ronald P. Kooser
Ronald J. Kruse
Paul D. Morrill

OKLAHOMA
    Richard C. McCleary

PENNSYLVANIA
    William Bohnet
    Glenn B. Bush
    James A. Davidson
    Robert G. Hoernig
    James W. Kee
    Robert C. Kline
    Thomas A. Longo
    John L. Manning
    John C. Mason
    James K. McFarland
    William J. Merz
    Edmund J. Schenck, Jr.
    Thomas A. Spowart, Jr.
    Howard W. Stringert

TEXAS
    Alvin W. Anderson
    Franklin J. Clements
    W. B. "Pick" Holmes
    Richard C. McCleary
    H. G. (Gene) Rice
    Donald J. Spilger

VIRGINIA
    Joel D. Griffing, Jr.

WISCONSIN
    Thomas H. Jaeschke

CANADA
    J. A. Jacques
    Beauchemin

Stuart L. Bellingham   Mario Kent L'Esperance
Gertrude Bernard   James Herbert Little
Gary R. Butts   Keith Little
Jean C. Guenette   William W. Lowrie
Nelson E. Hofer   Peter A. Moll
Paul F. Johnston   John W. Price
                            A. J. Waldhart

B. RESTAURANT ASSOCIATIONS

In addition to the National Restaurant Association, almost every state has its own association or affiliate. Each of these is ready and willing to provide a wide variety of assistance, pamphlets, training films, and information to help solve problems and assist in the educational field.

Alabama State Restaurant Association
Milton R. Durrett, Executive Secretary
1350 Brown Marx Building
Birmingham, Ala. 35203

California State Restaurant Association
Robert M. Riley, General Manager
448 South Hill St.
Los Angeles, Calif. 90013

Arizona Restaurant Association
Joe Banks, Executive Secretary
112 North Central
Phoenix, Ariz. 85004

Colorado-Wyoming Restaurant Association
Richard E. Carlton, Executive Secretary
1239 Elati St.
Denver, Colo. 80204

Arkansas Restaurant Association
Ray B. Thomas, Executive Secretary
907 Rector Building
Little Rock, Ark. 72201

Associated Restaurants of Connecticut
Lee Isenberg, Executive Director
179 Allyn St.
Hartford, Conn. 06103

Delaware Restaurant
Association
Robert Piane, President
P.O. Box 1705
Wilmington, Del. 19899

Restaurant Association of
Metropolitan
Washington, Inc.
John S. Cockrell, Executive
Vice-President
1147 20th St., N.W.
Washington, D.C. 20036

Florida Restaurant
Association
Jerome Robinson, Executive
Vice-President
1077 N.E. 125th St.
North Miami, Fla. 33161

Georgia Restaurant
Association
Edward P. England, Execu-
tive Vice-President
1401 Rhodes-Haverty
Building
Atlanta, Ga. 30303

Hawaii Restaurant
Association
Zaida Male, Executive
Secretary
2003 Kalia Road
Honolulu, Hawaii 96815

Idaho Restaurant and
Beverage Association
E. S. Middlemist, Executive
Secretary
2909 Madison Ave.
Boise, Idaho 83702

Chicago and Illinois Restau-
rant Association
Larry C. Buckmaster,
Executive Director
30 West Monroe St.
Chicago, Ill. 60603

Indiana Restaurant
Association
Warren Spangle, Executive
Vice-President
2120 North Meridian St.
Indianapolis, Ind. 46202

Iowa Restaurant Association
Peter C. Canakes, Executive
Vice-President
204 Shops Building
Des Moines, Iowa 50309

Kansas Restaurant
Association
W. T. Morris, Executive
Vice-President
359 South Hydraulic
Wichita, Kan. 67211

Kentucky Restaurant
Association, Inc.
Bill Thompson, Executive
Vice-President
202 West Chestnut St.
Louisville, Ky. 40402

Louisiana Restaurant
Association
Maurice Lewis, Executive
Vice-President
1626 International Trade
Mart Building
New Orleans, La. 70130

Maine Restaurant
Association
Ira D. Turner, Executive
Secretary
11 Maplewood St.
Portland, Me. 04103

Restaurant Association of
Maryland, Inc.
Mrs. Letitia B. Carter,
Executive Secretary
8 Charles Plaza
Baltimore, Md. 21201

Massachusetts Restaurant
Association
Raymond J. Murgia, Execu-
tive Vice-President
825 Washington St.
Newtonville, Mass. 02160

Michigan Restaurant
Association
Harold C. Gant, Executive
Vice-President
30215 Southfield Road
Southfield, Mich. 48075

Minnesota Restaurant
Association, Inc.
W. J. Bohr, Executive
Secretary
112 North Seventh St.
Minneapolis, Minn. 55403

Mississippi Restaurant
Association, Inc.
Roy Bailey, Executive
Vice-President
201 Primos-Fondren Building
Jackson, Miss. 39216

Missouri Restaurant
Association
Max Koerner, Executive
Vice-President
2 West 40th St.
Kansas City, Mo. 64111

Montana Restaurant
Association
M. E. Evanson, Executive
Secretary
Box 680
Billings, Mont. 59103

Nebraska Restaurant
Association
Herman Siefkes, Business
Manager
720 Lincoln Building
Lincoln, Neb. 68508

Granite State Restaurant
Association
Malcolm Stevenson,
Secretary
P.O. Box 157
Bethlehem, N.H. 03574

New Jersey Restaurant
Association
Frank M. Barrett, Executive
Director
Menlo Park Station
Box 2187
Edison, N.J. 08817

New Mexico Restaurant
Association
Howard Cowper, Executive
Director
414 San Mateo N.E.
Albuquerque, N.M. 87108

New York State Restaurant
Association, Inc.
Fred Sampson, Executive
Vice-President
369 Lexington Ave
New York, N.Y. 10017

North Carolina Restaurant
Association, Inc.
Mrs. T. Jerry Williams,
Executive Vice-
President
P.O. Box 6026
Raleigh, N.C. 27608

North Dakota Food and
Lodging Association
Ernest A. Benser, Executive
Secretary-Treasurer
1706 East Blvd.
Bismarck, N.D. 58501

Ohio State Restaurant
Association
Robert L. Henry, Executive
Secretary
40 South Third St.
Columbus, Ohio 43215

Oklahoma Restaurant
Association
Justin Hill, Executive
Director
2207 North Broadway
Oklahoma City, Okla. 73103

Restaurants of Oregon
Association
Mrs. Helen Riley Cover,
Executive Secretary
1228 S.W. Morrison
Portland, Ore. 97214

Pennsylvania Restaurant
Association
John D. Bolduc, Executive
Director
101 Locust St.
Harrisburg, Pa. 17101

Rhode Island Restaurant
Association
Gerald Hanley, Jr., Execu-
tive Secretary
1070 Main St.
Warren, R.I. 02885

South Carolina Restaurant
Association
W. W. Rogers, Executive
Director
2126 Devine St.
Columbia, S.C. 29205

South Dakota Restaurant
Association
Florence Holton, Secretary
P.O. Box 328
Sioux Falls, S.D. 57101

Tennessee Restaurant
Association
J. W. Turner, Executive
Vice-President
701 J. C. Bradford Building
Nashville, Tenn. 37219

Texas Restaurant
Association
W. Price, Jr., Executive
Vice-President
P.O. Box 1429
Austin, Texas 78767

Utah State Restaurant
Association
Wilford M. Burton, Execu-
tive Secretary
500 Kennecott Building
Salt Lake City, Utah 84111

Vermont Restaurant
Association
Berkeley V. Bennett, Execu-
tive Secretary
Box F
Stowe, Vt. 05672

Virginia Restaurant
Association
Walter F. Witt, Executive
Vice-President
2101 Libbie Ave.
Richmond, Va. 23230

Restaurant Association of the
State of Washington,
Inc.
Jack Gordon, Executive Vice-
President
220 Securities Building
Seattle, Wash. 98101

West Virginia Restaurant
Association
Louise B. Miragliotta, Execu-
tive Secretary
P.O. Box 2391
Charleston, W. Va. 25328

Wisconsin Restaurant
Association
Elmer Conforti, Executive
Vice-President
626 N. Van Buren
Milwaukee, Wis. 53202

C. ASSOCIATIONS OF THE INDUSTRY

Following is a complete list of the associations in the
food service industry and where to contact them.

American Hotel & Motel
Association
888 Seventh Ave.
New York, N.Y. 10019
*Executive Vice-President:
Lawson A. Odde*

American Restaurant China
Council
1850 East Las Tuna Rd.
Santa Barbara, Calif. 93103
*Executive Director: William
D. Christopher*

American School Food
Service Association
P.O. Box 10095
Denver, Colo. 80901
*Executive Director: John N.
Perryman*

Food Equipment Manufac-
turers Association
33 North LaSalle Street
Suite 3200
Chicago, Ill. 60602
Tel.: 312-RA 6-4300
*General Counsel: Frank J.
Madden*

Food Facilities Consultants
Society
135 Glenlawn Avenue
Sea Cliff, N.Y. 11579
*Executive Director: Henry
H. Rothman*

Food Service Equipment
Industry, Inc.
332 South Michigan Avenue
Chicago, Ill. 60604
Tel.: 312-427-9605
*Executive Director: Jess C.
Marshall*

International Foodservice
Manufacturers
Association
One East Wacker Drive
Chicago, Ill. 60601
Tel.: 312-467-0810
*Executive Vice-President:
Reuben R. Cordova*

International Society of Food
Service Consultants
Fabricators Div., Dallas
Sheet Metal Works
3004 Irving Boulevard
Dallas, Tex. 75247
Tel.: 214-631-6820
Joseph H. Berger

Manufacturers Agents for the
Food Service
Industry
1517 North Second Street
P.O. Box 1238
Harrisburg, Pa. 17108
Tel.: 717-234-7069
*Executive Secretary: Arthur
B. Olian*

National Association of Food
Equipment
Manufacturers
111 East Wacker Drive
Chicago, Ill. 60601
Tel.: 312-644-6610
*Executive Secretary: William
W. Carpenter*

National Restaurant
Association
1530 North Lake Shore Drive
Chicago, Ill. 60610
Tel.: 312-787-2525
*Director of Communications:
Charles Sandler*

National Sanitation
Foundation
P.O. Box 1468
Ann Arbor, Mich. 48106
Tel.: 313-663-8581
*Executive Director: Charles
A. Farish*

Permanent Ware Institute
Suite 1475
20 N. Wacker Drive
Chicago, Ill. 60606
Contact: Irwin Simms

D. TRADE PUBLICATIONS

There is a wide variety of regularly published magazines and papers that are a most valuable source of news on what is happening in the industry—surveys, studies, new equipment, recipes, foods, ideas, systems—all available to the student and those already engaged in the industry. Each school should get copies of these publications and use them to supplement the regular texts and courses. It is important to relate to what is going on in the industry now.

Cahners Publishing Co., Inc.
5 South Wabash Avenue
Chicago, Ill. 60603

Institutions Volume Feeding
Food Service Equipment Dealer
Service World International

Harcourt Brace Jovanovich Publications
757 Third Avenue
New York, N.Y. 10017

Food Management
Drive-in Fast Service
Quick Frozen Foods

Nation's Restaurant News
2 Park Avenue
New York, N.Y. 10016

Food and Equipment Product News
A Young/Conway Publication
347 Madison Avenue
New York, N.Y. 10017

E. BOOKS

The author of this text has written four books in recent years relating directly to the food service industry:

Planning and Operating a Successful Food Service Operation. New York: Chain Store Publishing Corporation.

Food Service on a Budget. Boston: Cahners Books, (1974). Schools, senior citizens, colleges, nursing homes, hospitals, industrial, correctional institutions.

Meeting Challenges in Food Service. New York: Chain Store Publishing Corporation, 1974.

The Food Service Productivity & Profit Handbook. Boston: Cahners Books, 1974.

Catalogs giving complete lists of books relating to the food service industry can be obtained from a number of publishers:

Prentice-Hall, Inc.
Englewood Cliffs, N.J. 07632

Chain Store Publishing Corp.
2 Park Avenue
New York, N.Y. 10016

AVI Publishing Company, Inc.
P.O. Box 831, 250 East State Street
Westport, Conn. 06880

Cahners Books
Cahners Publishing Corp.
89 Franklin Street
Boston, Mass. 02110

Index

A

B

C